DEADLY KIN

A True Story of
Mass Family Murder

ROBERT W. NEWSOM III
WILLIAM R. TROTTER

Insanity is having one too many bad ideas

—Kurt Vonnegut, Jr., *The Sirens of Titan*

There will be time, there will be time to prepare a face to meet the faces that you meet;. There will be time to murder and create ...

—T.S. Eliot, *The Love Song of J. Alfred Prufrock*

Published by arrangement with Signal Research, Inc.

DEADLY KIN

Copyright © 1988 by Signal Research, Inc.

ISBN: 0-312-91549-7   Can. ISBN: 0-312-91550-0

Printed in the United States of America

Piedmont Impressions edition published 1988
First St. Martin's Press mass market edition/June 1989

10 9 8 7 6 5 4 3 2 1

TABLE OF CONTENTS

Introduction

On July 22, 1984, in Prospect, Kentucky, a mysterious killer with a military-style assault rifle viciously murdered a 68-year-old woman and her 39-year-old daughter. The cold efficiency of the slayings and the lack of an obvious motive left Kentucky investigators baffled for months.

Unfortunately, these murders were merely the opening act in a tragic drama that didn't end until a year later with a fierce submachine-gun battle in Greensboro, North Carolina. Before it was all over, nine people died horrible, violent deaths, and three police officers were wounded. All of the murder victims were related by blood or marriage, and they spanned four generations of this extended family.

As police from several law enforcement agencies in two states closed in on the suspected killer, a member of a prominent family, they discovered that his primary goal in life was to become a doctor — a healer. Too late, they learned that he was also a heavily armed, disturbed young man who for years had been struggling with the failures in his life by seeking refuge in his vision of the apocalypse.

This is a story of murder and madness, of mayhem and death. The victims were killed with weapons ranging from an assault rifle and cyanide capsules to a bayonet and a bomb. This book — the culmination of 15 months of research — pulls no punches as it documents both the destruction of a family and the effects on the survivors. To add a personal perspective, some of the chapters are written by Robert W. Newsom III, a Greensboro attorney who lost four members of his family in the killings. Newsom's reflections are written from a first-person point of view and are identified at the beginning of each of his chapters.

CHAPTER ONE

The First Mission
Prospect, Kentucky, July 22, 1984

He had no trouble locating her house. He was quite good at reading maps. Besides, it had all been described to him, and he had an old snapshot ripped out of a scrapbook that no one looked at any more. In fact, the whole trip had been disappointingly easy.

After taking Interstate 65 into Louisville, all he had to do was drive north about fifteen miles, pick up State Road 329, then follow its winding path until he found the house. The properties that cover the rural landscape on both sides of the road are large and well groomed.

Now, through the trees, he sees enough of the houses to know that the people who live in them are not poor — they're the kind of people who, when they talk about "the farm," always seem to put the words in quotation marks. He does not have a whole lot of use for people like that. He has relatives like that himself. Too many of them. The Old Witch is one of those people, too.

He parks the Blazer under cover, where it can't be seen by anyone passing along the main road, and far enough from the objective so that anyone stumbling across it will not immediately connect it with that place. He doesn't mind walking some distance through the woods. If she went to the early church services as usual, he has plenty of time to accomplish what he came here to do.

The approach march clears his head, filling his lungs with the scents of a cool summer morning in the woods. Some of his best memories are of such smells, of just the kind of early-morning dappled sunlight now warming his face. He's young and strong and this is his first mission.

Staying deep under the tree shadows, he parallels the course of a long asphalt driveway and crosses over a small creek. Carefully, he avoids wet soil that might hold a bootprint. He stays in shallow water, then on dew-damp grass which, when it dries, will not reveal that he stalked here.

He pauses to remove from a case his .223-caliber Colt AR-15 assault rifle. The barrel and receiver glide together and hit with that incisive metallic clunk that he has always regarded as one of the most satisfying of sounds. He inserts a full magazine, lets the bolt carry the first round into the chamber, and sets the safety. Do it by the numbers. One-two-three, down the mental checklist that has been running through his mind all night long. Balanced now by the cantilevering weight of the firearm, he feels complete, powerful, and full of purpose. He has a new resolve, even a touch of swagger in his gait as he moves on toward the house.

It's as big as he had expected: two stories, built into a hillside slope surrounded by a chain-link fence, brick-walled, your basic upper-middle-class ranch house in the country. He sees two cars in the driveway parking loop, but her car isn't there. Another item gets ticked off on his checklist. He glances at his watch. The church service ought to be letting out soon. He's not sure how long it will take her to drive back, but he doesn't mind waiting.

He follows the shadows to a vantage point close to the parked cars. It's just like the old bat to have more cars than she could ever use. He knows how well fixed she is after the death of her husband. How much money she has to buy steak scraps for her dog! How much money she has to throw around on legal fees and airplane tickets!

He studies the house for any signs of life. He doesn't like surprises, but he thinks he can handle any that might arise. A car approaches, purring slowly up the long driveway. It's one of those family-style, smugly complacent models, gliding smoothly through

4

the early sunlight. A jolt of recognition surges through him as the woman's silhouette precisely matches the outline he's imprinted on his mind. It's her, all right.

She parks her car and gets out. He recognizes the owlish glasses, the prim, schoolmarm pinch of her mouth, a tartness in her smile — just as she looks in the old photo, complete with the sharp, self-righteous jut of her chin. How tiny she is. Five feet at the most. He rethinks the parameters of the shot he's planned.

Back turned toward him now, she fumbles for a key and starts to insert it in the door between the two closed panels of the garage. It's time. He'll never get a better shot. While her attention is focused on the door, he scuttles forward swiftly and silently, taking a position between two cars. He's close enough to count the wrinkles in her clothing. The sights come together, ring-and-blade, and it is as though a zoom lens has suddenly brought her close enough to touch. He sees the weave of the cloth, aims at the interstices of its fibers. Deep breath. Squeeze.

A solid small-caliber, high-velocity thump against his shoulder. A little puff of blood, like red dust, shoots from her back. She begins to sink to her knees, in slow motion, just like in the movies, crying out with a strange raspy moan. He can feel the waves of her pain and astonishment. It must seem to her as if God has reached down and flicked her with a thumb and forefinger, the way you'd pop a bug off your shirtsleeve.

Compensating for the recoil, he lowers the sights just a hair, and doesn't have to raise them because she's sinking. She seems to be on the verge of finding enough air for a real shriek. The stock slaps his cheek once more. Pieces of her skull — the images are swimming in adrenalized slow motion — seem to unwind like a scarlet turban. As she slumps awkwardly to the asphalt, there can be no doubt about it: the wicked Witch is dead. Surprised at how calm he is, he carefully picks up both empty shell casings and stuffs them into his pocket.

Someone is screaming. There's a pretty, dark-haired woman in jogging shorts, looking at him and screaming. She's at the top of a small flight of stone steps, at a gate that leads to the back yard. After the initial shock, his training kicks in and he begins to process this new data. Every operation has its surprises. The Witch was supposed to be alone here, but one of the marks of the professional is how well he can handle the overlooked or the accidental. Remember that copy of Von Clauswitz in Father's library — remember what the great German theoretician had said: "War is the provence of Chance."

Back in control now, he swings around and faces the screaming woman. She stares at him in horror, as if to say *Who are you? Why have you done this to my mother?* He springs at her. She throws one terrified glance at him as she sprints across the patio that runs along the rear of the house. There's a tense, athletic curve to her legs. Fifteen feet from the gate, he hoists the rifle and pops off a round. A small geyser of blood shoots from her back — a lung-shot, by the look of it. The high-velocity round has gone all the way through her and nicked the brick wall on her left.

Somehow she keeps going, lurching now through the back door, leaving a ragged trail of blood on the patio. He knows she'll die soon, but he has to make sure she doesn't get to a phone first. Leaping into the kitchen, he sees that she's already got the receiver in her hand. He comes up behind her, close enough to grab her. She turns and looks at him in horror, drops the receiver, and wobbles around the Formica counter. The door into the next room is blocked by some sort of dog-gate. He hears yapping and yowling, but he knows about these dogs — two Yorkshire terriers, no threat to him or the mission.

Carefully, so as not to tear his clothing and leave any trace of thread, he climbs over the gate and sees both dogs crouching in a corner, frenzied but impotent. He tunes out their racket. Following the trail of blood through the house, he goes through the den and into a hall. She's still shrieking. She's frantically trying to do something inside a closet in the hall. She panics when she sees him again and runs through the nearest open door. He takes his time. She's run out of places to hide. He pauses to inspect the closet and smiles when he sees the alarm mounted inside, against the wall, untriggered. She had been too paralyzed from pain and fear.

She runs through a bedroom into the bright lemony light of a glassed-in sunroom — a room with no door to the outside. He stands in the doorway and she looks up at him with an expression that fills him with a sense of potency. She should know, by now, that God is on *his* side of the trigger this morning. She crouches as he calmly approaches and sights on the curve of her neck. He watches plastic hair curlers bobbing along the base of her skull and fires once, the impact driving one of the curlers into the wound. It protrudes like some weird kind of tuber. The woman's body shudders and goes still.

Methodically, he retraces his steps back through the house and outside to the driveway, gathering up the brass shell casings ejected by his rifle. Walking back to his car, the woods seem drenched in beauty. He feels vital, proven. Mission accomplished.

CHAPTER TWO

Dies Irae
Prospect, Kentucky, July 1984

When Delores and Charles Lynch first met in Pittsburgh just before World War II, Charles was an executive-level engineer with General Electric. They married and had two children, Jane and Tom. The family's early years were nomadic as Charles was transferred from city to city. Eventually, while Tom, the younger child, was attending college, Delores and Charles moved to the rural town of Prospect, Kentucky, some fifteen miles north of Louisville. Charles Lynch died in 1983, leaving an estate valued in press accounts at more than two million dollars.

Though she could be generous to her children, Delores was notoriously stingy with everyone else — except her dogs, who ate steak scraps while Delores collected pennies-off coupons for her grocery shopping. By the spring of 1984, Delores had become deeply involved in her son Tom's custody fight, helping to defray some of the costs involved in his lengthy campaign to regain partial custody of his boys from their mother, Susie Newsom Lynch, whom Delores disliked intensely.

Delores was a willful and opinionated woman. If she liked you, or what you were doing, she said so. If she didn't like you or what you were doing, she made no effort to disguise it. She spoke her mind bluntly, to your face.

Her daughter, Jane Lynch, an attractive and steady young woman, had a Masters degree and had worked as a speech therapist for some years in California before returning to the University of Kentucky at

Lexington to attend dental school. She had graduated that spring and was planning to stay with her mother until she decided where to set up practice. She had been living with Delores only a few days before July 22, 1984.

The bodies of Delores and Jane Lynch were discovered by a family friend on Tuesday, July 24, 1984. Delores was found near the place where she had parked her car after returning from church on Sunday. Most of her head had been blown off and she was lying at the end of a 30-foot-long stream of blood.

Jane Lynch, 39, was found inside the house, where she had attempted to flee from her assailant. She had been hit first with a shot in the back which tore through her lungs. Then she had been finished at close range with a coup de grace at the base of her skull.

The first lawman to reach the scene was Chief Steve Nobles of the Oldham County Police Department. His brother, Lynn Nobles, was later assigned to the team that tried to crack the case. It was Lynn's first murder case, and one he would remember for a long time.

The man in charge of the Kentucky investigation was Lieutenant Dan Davidson, a tough-talking, rangy veteran of thirty years' police work, including some rough-and-tumble tours in Harlan County. Davidson came from a family with a long tradition of police work. His father had been a sheriff, and Davidson had followed in his footsteps, first as a state trooper, and now as a detective. Davidson had seen it all during his career, from the flakiest crimes to the most brutal murders, but the KlennerNewsom killings would disturb him more than any other case he'd ever worked on.

The preliminary investigation of the Lynch murders left Davidson completely baffled. The Lynch house was chock-full of stealable, easily fenced stuff: jewelry, electronics, silverware, antiques — one trunkload of this kind of merchandise could set up the average burglar for a year of easy living. But nothing had been stolen. Some of Delores' things appeared to have been messed with a little, but none of the really valuable things had even been touched.

Moreover, the killings themselves were remarkably tidy. No spent shell casings, no fingerprints, and no obvious evidence of a wasted

10

shot. There was something chillingly methodical and planned-out about it. It looked like a "surgical strike." It looked, to Davidson, like nothing so much as a professional hit, though why anybody would want to put out a contract on a little old lady like Delores Lynch was hard to imagine. Davidson told the press that it looked like a robbery. What else could he tell them?

Tom Lynch, a successful dentist, was at his home in Albuquerque, New Mexico when he learned about the murders of his mother and sister. When the dreadful news was relayed to him, Tom had just returned from a fun-filled visit to a dude ranch with his two young children, Jim and John. It was one of the few chances he had to see his boys, because he had very limited visitation rights following his divorce from their mother, Susie Newsom Lynch, who lived in Greensboro, North Carolina. Distraught, Tom telephoned Susie in Greensboro and informed her of the murders. He asked if the boys could stay just a while longer with him in New Mexico, as their presence gave him comfort. Susie rebuffed him without so much as a word of sympathy or compassion.

But Susie was not as reticent later when she telephoned her lawyer, Sandy Sands. She told him that gangsters had snuffed the Lynches — she was certain of it — and that the attackers would probably now go after the two boys, out in New Mexico. It was somewhat curious that Susie talked about the murders in terms of a gangland hit. The Kentucky police were still describing the slayings as an interrupted robbery attempt.

Meanwhile, Susie's mother, Florence Newsom, who lived near Winston-Salem, North Carolina, wrote Tom Lynch a letter of condolence. Tom later replied with a desperate cry from the heart: Would she help him in his battle to gain the right to a decent amount of regular contact with his sons? Susie, he explained, refused to permit them to make any calls to their father. He received no letters, no school pictures, no packets of crayon drawings, none of those pathetic but treasurable little things that a divorced parent clutches at; those little talesmen that assure you that the kids are all right, and that they are growing up as kids ought to grow; little things that give some sense — however sparse — of what their daily routines are like.

Florence agreed that Tom deserved better treatment and that it would be good for the boys to see more of him. The alternative father figure was Susie's cousin and live-in companion, whom the boys called "Uncle Fritz." Florence considered Fritz quite unpalatable. The fact that the two boys now went to school dressed in camouflage outfits, just like those Fritz wore, filled her with a vague but powerful sense of dread, of something pervasively and profoundly out of balance. Unfortunately, Susie could not be reasoned with at that time, and Florence confessed that she no longer knew how to break through to her daughter.

When Tom Lynch arrived in Kentucky for the funerals, Lt. Davidson routinely questioned him in detail. It was the most logical thing to do, considering the size of Delores's estate and the fact that Tom would inherit everything. But apart from Tom's ironclad alibi — he had been in New Mexico on the day of the killings, and had plenty of witnesses to back him up — Davidson mentally struck Tom from his list of suspects almost at once. In his thirty years as a cop, Davidson had learned how to read people pretty well. He was sure within minutes of meeting Tom Lynch that the young man was incapable of killing his mother, his sister, or anybody else, for that matter.

Besides, an in-depth background check on Tom Lynch revealed no bad habits, no police record, no criminal connections. And Lynch had no trouble passing two lie detector tests.

For the next ten months, Davidson and his assistants checked out every possibility, ran down every tip that came in by phone, no matter how bizarre or ludicrous. But they came up with nothing. Not a whisper. Everything ended in thin air. It was the damndest case Davidson had ever worked on. It was almost as if a team of hit-men had parachuted into Prospect, Kentucky one morning, briskly iced their victims, and had then been lifted away in some unmarked helicopter and flown to a secret base in the mountains.

He didn't know it, but that kind of scenario had probably been flickering on the movie-screen inside the killer's mind: a deep penetration raid into enemy territory; a quick, surgical strike at the target; a smooth and trackless withdrawal. Mission accomplished.

CHAPTER THREE

Doctor Fred

Greensboro is the third-largest city in North Carolina, after Charlotte and the state capital, Raleigh. In the mid-1980s, Greensboro had about 160,000 residents, but the spacious city was spread out over an area fifty percent larger than Boston or San Francisco.

Unlike nearby Winston-Salem, Greensboro boasts no dominant corporation on the scale of tobacco giant R.J. Reynolds, although in its heyday, Cone Mills was a paternalistic presence. The city derives its prosperity from a concentration of financial businesses, distribution centers, and manufacturing — textiles and furniture, mainly, but with an increasing amount of high-technology activity. This middle-class economic base is complemented by half a dozen colleges and universities, the largest of which is the University of North Carolina at Greensboro. UNCG is a somnolent campus, but that very absence of ferment is among the qualities which draw numerous students to the place.

Greensboro has yet to make up its mind what sort of city it aspires to be (its forlorn downtown has been "revived" more times than a CPR practice dummy), but the nice thing is that nobody seems to be in any hurry about it. The cultural infrastructure is neither lavishly funded nor pretentious, but the recognized excellence of UNCG's graduate writing program, coupled with the city's laid-back ambience, have given it a literary reputation unique for a city so otherwise bereft of intellectual intensity. Turn over a rock anywhere within a five-mile radius of the university campus, and two or three pale scribblers will wriggle out into the sunlight.

Reidsville, North Carolina, located just twenty miles or so north of Greensboro, was founded in 1815 by a farmer named Reuben Reid. Technically speaking, Reidsville may be considered a suburb of Greensboro, but it has its own identity and cannot be regarded as just a bedroom community for its larger neighbor. Indeed, it is safe to predict that, when every other surrounding community has been absorbed by the future Triad megalopolis of Greensboro, Winston-Salem, and High Point, Reidsville will still be the same stubbornly individualistic little town it has always been.

To be sure, the place has more than its share of good ol' boy troglodytes, but it also has a reputation for producing eccentrics. Maybe it's something in the water. Find the most extreme, most opinionated, most soapbox-eloquent letter to the editor in the Sunday edition of the *Greensboro News and Record*, and chances are it's signed by somebody from Reidsville. Leathery Bible-whomping reactionaries thrive there, but so do cracker-barrel radicals, part-time poets, and philosophical mavericks who fiercely resist any facile categorization. This tradition dates back to Reidsville's wealthiest citizen, tobacco tycoon Jeff Penn, who dwelt in baronial splendor in a 27-room "English country house" just outside of town. So complete was Penn's proprietorship over Reidsville that, if the urge was upon him, he thought nothing of stopping on the sidewalk in the middle of town, opening his fly, and relieving himself into the street, nodding blithely at passersby as he did so. That's what the locals will tell you, anyway.

The locals will also tell you a lot of stories about Reidsville's most famous recent eccentric, Doctor Frederick Klenner. Most folks in Reidsville thought "ol' Doc Fred" was something special. It didn't matter that he was also kind of strange — every small town needs a prominent eccentric, and Doc made a fine one.

Doctor Frederick Klenner was the youngest son of a family of good, solid, German immigrants who had originally settled in Johnstown, Pennsylvania. His father worked himself literally to death in the steel mills so his son could go to medical school. But Fred first attended Catholic University in Washington, and for a time seems to have flirted quite seriously with the idea of becoming a priest.

He met his future wife, Annie Hill Sharp, during his second year at Duke Medical School. The Sharp family was dead set against their marriage from the beginning. But marry they did, in 1937.

Doctor Fred interned at the Forsyth County Sanitarium in 1939 and, following that taxing interlude, he gave in to his wife's urgings and went to Reidsville, where he hung out his shingle and opened a family practice on the second floor of a downtown office building. By the time his only son, Fritz, was born in 1952, Doctor Fred had been practicing medicine in Reidsville for thirteen years. He had also become a living landmark.

Shortly after World War II, Dr. Fred became deeply involved in the specialized field of orthomolecular medicine — in which common body chemicals, mainly vitamins, are deployed against a variety of illnesses, usually by means of massive doses injected directly into the patient's bloodstream.

Doctor Klenner's interest in therapeutic vitamin treatments began at home, when he cured his own wife's case of bleeding gums with some injections of vitamin C. After that experience, he started administering mega-doses of vitamin C for everything from measles to pneumonia; he published the first of many papers on the subject in the late 1940s.

He first attracted the sometimes-unkind attention of the medical profession in 1952 when he published claims of dramatic polio cures obtained, or at least triggered, by gigantic doses of vitamin C. It was this aspect of his research which earned him a favorable mention in Adelle Davis' trendy mid-Fifties best seller *Let's Eat Right to Keep Fit*. An even more prestigious accolade came in 1970, when Nobel Prize laureate Linus Pauling singled out Klenner as a "medical pioneer" in the pages of his controversial and enormously influential book, *Vitamin C and the Common Cold*.

After his early success with vitamin C, Klenner began working with the B vitamins, convinced that they were effective agents against multiple sclerosis — a thesis which the medical establishment found highly dubious. Word of his mega-vitamin treatments, however, did bring numerous MS patients to his Reidsville office. To

15

this day, there are a large number of people who swear that Doctor Fred's shots improved or even cured their MS.

By the mid-1950s, Doctor Fred had published studies claiming mega-vitamin cures for polio, multiple sclerosis, pneumonia, and a number of less threatening conditions. His cures, however, were based almost wholly on subjective observations made inside the walls of his own clinic, and he assumed the rest of the medical profession would simply take his word for it. When it was suggested that his word might carry greater weight if he had conducted his experiments in the classic and accepted control-group style, Doctor Klenner scoffed.

His critics in the American Medical Association (AMA) charged that Dr. Fred's "tests" were unacceptably subjective and that his presentation of data made both duplication and verification of his results impossible. His experiments, said the medical establishment, were not properly controlled; his results were skewed by openly subjective observations and criteria; his methodology was lax; and more than a few of his diagnoses were open to question. There were even some suggestions that his cures were as bad as the diseases. When one of his patients was stricken with brain edema, some of his local colleagues voiced the suspicion that the cause might be Doc's massive injections of vitamin A. Some of the dosages were indeed massive: One multiple sclerosis patient received as many as sixty-four injections a day.

Doctor Klenner was acutely conscious of the fact that his experiments and methods placed him on the borders of medical respectability. He returned this skepticism with contempt. He thought that the AMA contained a large number of fools, and he didn't hesitate to say so publicly on numerous occasions.

In 1960, he moved his practice into larger offices above what is now the Rite Aid drugstore on Gilmer Street in Reidsville. After a patient climbed the stairs and entered Doctor Klenner's office, he found himself not in a modern waiting room with color-coordinated furniture and a discreetly soothing selection of prints on beige walls, but rather in some whacked-out cartoonist's idea of what an old-time doctor's office might have looked like around 1890.

The occupant of the office fit the part. Doctor Fred Klenner was a tall, rangy man, whose face was dominated by a formidable, proud, nose and gentle, compassionate eyes. Even those patients who found his treatments disquieting found his bedside manner reassuring. He bore himself like a healer. There was always something powerfully patriarchal about his way of speaking to, or touching, a patient.

There are a thousand "Doctor Fred" yarns still in circulation in Reidsville. Sometimes he quoted scripture to his patients. Once in a while, he would anoint them with a liquid he identified as "holy water from Lourdes." Patients who didn't care for his style quickly made their exit, while those who did respond favorably to this spiritually inflected treatment tended not just to come back over and over again, becoming in some instances patients for life, but also to ascribe near-miraculous healing powers to him. These were the Klenner loyalists, and even today they regard ol' Doc as a kind of regional guru — a bit funny in his ways, perhaps, but these qualities were a function of his genius and dedication.

Let there be no question about it: Doctor Klenner helped a great many people, and he was an "old-fashioned doctor" in the best sense of the word. He would make house calls, he would make you feel as though you were receiving special, individual attention, and he would never dun a poor man for an overdue bill. In short, he dispensed the kind of compassion and personal concern that patients often yearn to find in their physicians but sometimes don't receive in today's assembly-line clinics.

Even Doctor Fred's black patients felt good about him — despite the fact that he maintained separate White and Colored waiting rooms until his death in 1984.

Black or white, a lot of people still speak about him in phrases of striking similarity: "He could make you feel better just by walking into the room. He could touch you, and you just knew, in your heart, that everything would turn out all right."

Bedside Manners

I want to be as fair as I possibly can to the memory of Doctor Klenner — after all, dummies do not graduate from Duke Medical School. The Sharps and the Newsoms never questioned Fred Klenner's creativity and brilliance in orthomolecular medicine. Most of us figured, well, hey, if he's important enough to be singled out by Linus Pauling, that's good enough for us. And most of us had a great deal of sympathy with Fred's notion that institutionalized medicine in this country is opposed to pioneering, individual efforts. At the same time, we all felt he brought a great deal of difficulty on himself by refusing to structure his research in the accepted way.

We all knew people with multiple sclerosis (diagnosed by other physicians, not by Fred Klenner) who had made remarkable progress under his care. Not all of his achievements in that area were puffery and illusion, and not all conventional physicians felt he was a quack. There were a number of reputable doctors in central North Carolina who referred their MS patients to Doctor Klenner as a sort of last-gasp effort, and who were very pleased at the progress those patients made — though whether you could get any of them to admit that publicly now is highly questionable.

I personally know of several people who experienced significant improvement or relief under Doctor Klenner's regimens. No one ever questioned that, just as no one ever questioned his dedication to his patients; that was very real, never faked. In Doctor Klenner, there was a mixture of darkness and light, with the light almost always prevailing. His son Fritz, unfortunately, inherited all the darkness.

Doc helped a lot of people who came to him in states of despair, when conventional therapies had done them no good. And, in contrast to any number of doctors I could name, he was genuinely uninterested in the monetary aspect of his practice. I knew some rich people in Houston, a city with one of the most advanced medical infrastructures in the world, who would fly to Greensboro, rent a car, and drive up to Reidsville to be treated by Fred Klenner. He could have charged those individuals ten or even twenty times as much as he did, and they would have paid without a squeak of protest. These were people who could just as easily have flown to some swank monkey-gland clinic in Switzerland if they'd wanted to, but instead they chose to go to Reidsville and get treated in this baroquely cluttered, little second-floor rabbit-warren of a clinic.

Now, none of this is to deny that the other side of the family didn't find plenty of amusement in some of Doc's peculiarities — his insistence on doing everything on a cash-only basis for example, or his archaic and highly personalized religious obsessions. It's easy to snicker at Fred's belief that some sort of vast, nebulous Jewish-Negro-Communist conspiracy was pulling the strings of Wall Street, the media, and the whole federal government; but to be fair about it, that kind of attitude could also be found on the Protestant side of the family.

Grandpa Sharp was a foot-washing, dunk-em-in-the-river Baptist who had absolutely no use for Papists. He could barely tolerate Anglicans, for that matter. When Fred Klenner suddenly appeared, asking for Annie Hill's hand in marriage, I can imagine the consternation. In fact, I heard tales about it all my life. Fred was first of all a Yankee, which was one strike against him that he might have overcome in time. But he was also a very devout and very primitive Catholic, and he was from immigrant stock to boot. German immigrants at that.

I suspect that the whole religious business was kept going by the Sharps as much as anyone. There is, in the rural South, a belief, every bit as medieval in its own way as Fred's Catholic mysticism, that there is some kind of Jesuit plot to take over the world. I know my mother was not entirely free of that. She was convinced that ninety percent of all Catholic dogma was superstitious rot foisted off on the ignorant to keep them enslaved to the Vatican and busy manufacturing little baby Catholics. Real crude Catholic-baiting stuff, of course, but Mother, when that mood was upon her, was neither discreet nor diplomatic in giving voice to her feelings.

Let me underscore that nothing petty or hurtful that may have been said within the ranks of the Sharps was ever meant to get back to the Klenners' ears. They were too mannerly to permit that. But snide remarks made on one side of a small town like Reidsville always have a way of getting back to the other side of town.

I'm sure there wasn't any one thing that caused all the resentment which eventually surfaced. It was just a lot of little things that got back to Fred and had the cumulative effect of making it clear to him that some of his in-laws regarded him as a second-class citizen.

Children have remarkable internal radar systems. I am dead certain that Fritz must have picked up on that underlying tension when he was a kid, and that he became increasingly aware of it as he got older. Especially the idea that his father was considered a little bit weird. And Fritz's identification with his father was so absolute that a snicker directed at Doc became a snicker directed at Fritz as well.

I suppose the best way to describe Doctor Klenner is to say that he was not really demented so much as just pervasively out of sync — with conventional politics, with conventional ethical thinking, with modern science itself. He was probably the last doctor in America to use one of those antique sterilizers instead of disposable needles. It would sit in the corner of his office, full of bluish liquid, bubbling like a hotdog steamer. All of his equipment was like that: serviceable but ancient.

I myself had occasion to get a few shots from Doc. By God, those shots hurt! The needles had so much mileage on them that the points had dulled. I'm sure that's why he kept the sterilizer, because he would have bankrupted himself if he'd used a new hypo every time, considering how many shots he gave. He even joked about it once when I was in the office, saying: "I'll bet I give more injections in a year than most physicians give in a lifetime."

21

His waiting room looked like the reception foyer at Lyndon LaRouche headquarters: stacks and stacks of literature about Communist plots, exposes of the United Nations, books on UFOs, political and economic tracts of various sorts, old copies of *None Dare Call It Treason*, back issues of *The American Rifleman*, and so forth.

His religious views, though passionately and deeply held, were also out of sync. His brand of Catholicism would have been in vogue about the time of Torquemada, and it was very heavy on the mystical side of things. Both Doctor Fred, and later, Fritz, were extremely interested in signs, omens, and portents. Doctor Klenner and I once talked at great length, for example, about the mystical symbolism of the stigmata. Doc told me he subscribed to the belief that the wounds of Christ could still appear on the hands and feet of those who attained a mystical intimacy with the state of agonized grace that Jesus knew on the cross. That particular set of beliefs peaked, I suppose, around the time of Saint Francis.

The type of Catholicism Fritz ended up with was definitely not modern. It was the kind of Catholicism you might find practiced by illiterate peasants in Transylvania. For example, not too many contemporary American Catholics wear scapulars (monastic garments that cover the shoulders and hang down toward the feet). Yet at the time when they were all living together in Greensboro, Fritz, my sister Susie, and her two boys were wearing the short version of those garments, the kind associated with "tertiary" religious orders — sects of people who live in the world, but who embrace monastic ideals and are allowed to participate in rites and privileges usually denied to those beyond the cloister walls. Of course, Fritz and Susie belonged to no official religious order, tertiary or otherwise, except the one Fritz had constructed for them from his own delusions.

Doc Klenner worked out most of his own private antisocial tendencies on the fringe areas of his daily activity, but once in a while the man's darker side broke through. It's common knowledge within the family, for instance, that on at least one occasion there was domestic violence in the Klenner household. And based on my experience as a trial lawyer, there is no such thing as "just one" such incident in a family's history.

There was room in Doctor Klenner's creed for an almost Sicilian sense of vendetta, too. In fact, there is a long history of get-backs between the families that dates from the night of my sister's birth.

There was this fellow in Reidsville — let's just call him "George" — who was a neighbor of my mother's family. He worshipped Doctor Klenner, often running little errands for him, taking care of little chores for him, that sort of thing. Turned out he was also the main conduit for gossip about what was said over at the Sharp house. Whatever he happened to overhear, he carried it right back to Fred. This came to light because Fred's receptionist was a distant kinswoman of the Sharps, and she sent word back up the street to the effect that, "You folks better watch what you say when George is around, because he's repeating every word of it to Fred." Typical small-town deep-throating and friendly neighborhood espionage.

The poor-mouthing really must have fermented in Fred, considering how he got back at Mother on the night Susie was born. Now, Mother wanted to have her first child at home, and quite naturally she asked Fred to be the attending physician.

Fred performed an episiotomy on Mother without any anesthetic. He did it on purpose, and it caused her untold needless agony. I know he did it on purpose because he later bragged about it to George. It was an act of cold-blooded sadism. I don't know of any other way to describe it. Fred managed to con my parents by giving them some kind of medical mumbo-jumbo explanation which my father perforce had to accept.

If it had been my wife, I'd have decked the son of a bitch.

23

CHAPTER FIVE

They Won't Bother Us Again

Fritz Klenner grew up in a household where stifling love commingled with unreal expectations. Doctor Fred was his son's only close friend. Except for relatives, other kids simply weren't allowed into the house. If they had gone inside, they would surely have been intrigued by what they found, for Fred Klenner was an accumulator. In private life, he was comfortable only when surrounded by walls of collected, hoarded, cached, agglomerated *stuff*. The Klenner house, which was on the dark and labyrinthine side to begin with, was crammed full: tottering piles of books, papers, journals, correspondence, pamphlets, a horde of old clocks, bits and pieces of machinery, medical equipment, pharmaceutical samples, phonograph records, files, clothing, *objects d'art* nested on the same shelf with tacky bric-a-brac. And guns. Lots of guns.

When Fred took Fritz to the family farm, a heavily wooded 256-acre tract on the Dan River, near Eden, North Carolina, they did a lot of shooting together. Oddly, Fritz was only a fair rifle shot, but he was a truly superb pistol marksman, which is much less common. That made his father very proud.

They also blasted a lot of holes into the landscape with dynamite. Doctor Fred was convinced that the land under his property was honeycombed with lava-bores and mysterious caverns. He wanted to blow an entrance into that underground world so he and Fritz could

25

explore it together. Now and then, he also enlisted Fritz's help in stalking the "Bigfoot" creature who lived, Doc was certain, in the deep woods nearby. Father and son sometimes made casts of "footprints" and collected specimens of droppings, then sent them off to the Smithsonian Institution.

That the Smithsonian coolly acknowledged his offerings without immediately dispatching a field team to the Klenner property only proved what Doctor Fred already knew: The Communists had infiltrated every level of the government and were on the verge of overthrowing Western civilization. The Communists were going to sponsor a rebellion by the Negroes, Doc told Fritz, recounting his favorite apocalyptic scenario. When that happened, Armageddon would be at hand. It would most certainly come to pass, and it might happen very soon. If you studied the matter, he insisted, it was possible to discern the signs of the gathering storm. When he really got wound up about the subject, Doctor Klenner intimated that he even had foreknowledge of the exact date. When Fritz asked him to share that bit of arcane wisdom, Doctor Klenner would say, "You don't really want to know," implying that the burden of such knowledge was not for the young.

Fred was, in short, a True Believer: in segregation, in the John Birch Society, in UFOs, in the idea that Hitler was the victim of nefarious underlings and bad press, and in the efficacy of vitamins to cure polio.

And all of this was simmering in the same psychological stewpot with that extraordinary strain of medieval Catholicism. One night, when Doctor Klenner was preparing to go out on a house call, he claimed he heard strange noises upstairs. When a search failed to reveal any visible cause, he announced his verdict in one word: "Spooks!" Then he systematically exorcised the room, standing in the doorway and flinging dollops of holy water into the darkness. This completed, he confidently announced: "They won't bother us again."

To celebrate Fritz's entry into the seventh grade, Doctor Klenner presented his son with a German Luger.

CHAPTER SIX

Blood Ties

There are many people who regard Winston-Salem as the prettiest city in North Carolina's "Triad" — a triangular urban concentration in the northern Piedmont, defined, at its other two angles, by Greensboro and High Point. All three cities are inching toward one another, year by year, like reluctant amoebas, and developers talk about a time in the early 21st century when there will be a united Triad incorporating all three cities.

Maybe so, but the odds are that Winston-Salem will be the last leg of that triangle to compromise any of its individual identity. Winston is a wealthy city, graced by long, green, hilly avenues of solid, prosperous homes. The city boasts one of the most culturally active upper-middle classes to be found anywhere in the state. Site of the fabled North Carolina School of the Arts, the handsome and progressive Southeastern Center for Contemporary Art, and the vast resources of Wake Forest University, Winston-Salem is given to patting itself on the back, and not without justification.

The money that engendered all these things came mainly from the city's long association with "The Company." The R.J. Reynolds Tobacco Company first started churning out cigarettes there in 1875. Over the decades since, a lot of symphony concerts and art exhibits have owed their very existence to tobacco money. You can see the whole Reynolds symbiosis enshrined as well as encapsulated at Reynolda House, the majestic, 125-acre mansion of the Reynolds family. Now open to the public, the Reynolda House contains an important collection of American art, and its elegant, balconied living room is the site of frequent chamber music concerts.

The more distant past is lovingly preserved in Old Salem, the most ancient section of Winston-Salem. This community was settled in the 18th century by the gentle and civilized Moravians, who were composing string quartets at a time when the rest of America was still listening to tom-toms. Flanking the restored 18th-century settlement of Old Salem is the vast, rolling expanse of the old Moravian graveyard. Within this necropolis of beauty and serenity, three centuries' worth of citizens rest beneath towering trees, and the monumental rococo tombs of millionaires hulk next to the humble gravestones of 19th-century children.

Hattie Newsom lived just a few miles north of Reynolda House, not far past the entrance to the Wake Forest campus, at 3239 Valley Road in the lush, green Winston-Salem suburb of Old Town. Hattie was a Moravian, but in 1919 she had married a Presbyterian, Robert Newsom Sr. Although at the time this was definitely considered a "mixed marriage," Hattie and Robert each went to separate churches all their lives without any discernable strain on their relationship.

The couple had purchased the house on Valley Road in Old Town back in the 1930s. It was a large, solid manse of a house, set well back from Valley Road in a yard shaded by patriarchal oaks. Portions of the structure dated back to the Civil War, and it still had a definite antebellum look about it: a big rocking-chair porch and a set of classic white columns. After extensive remodeling, Hattie and Robert moved into the house in 1943. At that time, this part of Forsyth County outside Winston-Salem was pure piedmont countryside. When Reynolda Road was cut through the area, one-third of the Valley Road property had been sectioned off for the construction. Still, even though you could dimly hear the traffic and could sometimes glimpse it through the greenery that surrounded their home, Hattie and Robert's little four-acre estate remained comfortably pastoral.

Robert, a Winston-Salem native, had held any number of knockabout jobs before his marriage, but afterwards he settled down and went to work for R.J. Reynolds. He was no stranger to the tobacco business; his father had been a tobacco auctioneer. Lured by the same prospect of becoming his own boss, Robert went into business for himself. He was a hard worker with a natural aptitude for tobacco, and by the time he sold out his share in the Carolina Star Warehouse in 1973, he was financially secure.

In his last years, Robert Newsom Sr. took deep, quiet pride in the size and strength of the family he had seen grow up around him during his long life. Family members called him "Paw Paw," and they called Hattie "Nana." A man of boundless good humor, fond of games and jokes, well-liked and respected, Paw Paw Newsom died in 1980 at the age of 82. Widowed, Hattie lived alone in the big house at 3239 Valley Road.

But in 1984, more remodeling was under way. Hattie and Robert's son, Robert Newsom Jr., and his wife Florence, had decided that Nana, now 85 and burdened with a mild heart condition, should not live alone any longer. Now that Robert Jr. and Florence were themselves retired, they had decided to move in with Nana, and the Valley Road home was being altered to accommodate them. The target date for their move was at the end of July 1984, as soon as the work had been completed. Often on weekends, Robert Jr. and Florence would drive over from Greensboro and spend the weekend with Hattie, not so much out of obligation as simple affection.

Not that Hattie was a lonely old widow; she had many friends. A small woman with a fine, eager laugh, she was still independent; still drove herself around. She was extremely active at her church, Bethabara Moravian, where she had taught Sunday school for forty years. She baked great chicken pies, tended a large and verdant garden, and made Moravian cookies by the bushel each Christmas. Children instinctively felt at ease with her and gave her their trust, for she was kindly and never too busy to listen to what they had to say. Her zest for living was obvious and other people drew inspiration from it. Still, despite Hattie's active lifestyle, Robert Jr. and Florence felt it was best for her not to continue living alone. Besides, Robert Jr. wanted to spend his retirement years in Winston-Salem, a city he'd always loved.

Robert Newsom Jr. was a graduate of North Carolina State University. When World War II erupted, he served in the Merchant Marine during the Battle of the North Atlantic. "I didn't mind getting shot at for my country," he declared at the end of the war, "but I'm real glad I didn't have to shoot back at anyone."

After his tours of duty on the convoy routes, Bob Jr. returned home. While giving a speech about the Merchant Marine at a high school in Winston-Salem, he met, and fell in love with, an attractive young business teacher named Florence Sharp, who hailed from Reidsville. They were married in 1945 and settled in Old Town, not far from the Valley Road home of his parents, Robert Sr. and Hattie Newsom. Like his father, Bob Jr. began his career at R.J. Reynolds. Florence taught classes in what is now North Forsyth Senior High.

Florence Sharp Newsom came from one of the most prominent families in the town of Reidsville. Her father, James Sharp, was a respected lawyer in the area for many years and was eventually elected to the State Senate. Florence was the next-to-youngest of the ten Sharp children. She attended Women's College in Greensboro (now the University of North Carolina at Greensboro) and had embarked on a teaching career, first at a high school in Kings Mountain and then at Hanes High School in Winston-Salem. It was at Hanes High that she met Robert Newsom Jr. during his speaking engagement on behalf of the Merchant Marine.

Bob Jr. and Florence soon had two children: Susie Sharp Newsom, born in 1947; and Robert W. Newsom III, born in 1949.

Florence's oldest sister, Susie Sharp, followed her father into both the legal profession and the state's Democratic Party apparatus. Soon she became the first female Superior Court judge in North Carolina history. She topped that by becoming the first woman ever to be appointed to the North Carolina Supreme Court, and finally capped her career by becoming Chief Justice — the first woman in America to be made chief justice of a state supreme court. It was a high enough honor to land her on the cover of *Time* magazine, and it solidified the Sharps as a prominent local family.

Another of Florence's sisters was Anne Sharp, whom everyone called "Annie Hill." Annie earned a nursing degree from Duke University and eventually married an eccentric doctor from Reidsville named Frederick Klenner Sr.

So this was the connection, the blood-tie between the Sharps and the Klenners: Annie Hill's marriage to Doctor Klenner joined the families, and eventually made Susie Newsom and Fritz Klenner first cousins.

But when Susie and Fritz would eventually become drawn and bound together, the attractive force between them would be much more than a simple family relationship. It would be something darker, stranger, and at its core filled with unfathomable secrets.

Cousinly Visits

Doctor Klenner's house was a great place to visit when I was a kid. I used to look forward to going there. Kids feel comfortable in a messy place. We weren't allowed to play outside without supervision, because Doctor Klenner believed that if you played in the front yard, someone might come by and kidnap you. But inside the house it was kind of nice. Doc had all this neat stuff piled around, creating all these interesting, womb-like nooks and crannies.

Of all the nephews and nieces, my sister Susie was unquestionably Doc's favorite; you could see that even when she was a small child. I believe the affection was genuine and I believe she probably returned it.

But when we were children, I spent a lot more time with Fritz than Susie did. She was six years older than Fritz and there wasn't a whole lot they would have had in common as children. I don't recall any problems in my relationship with Fritz, but it was not especially close and soul-sharing, even as we grew into adolescence.

We often talked about guns because a fondness for firearms was one of the things we shared. But even there, the overlap was generic rather than specific, because all of my fantasies had to do with big-game hunting, and Fritz was always more interested in the military and the quasi-military. I used to daydream about being rich enough to own a customized Mannlicher or something equally classy, but Fritz's fetish was submachine guns. He was a firepower freak rather than a sportsman.

In our high school years, my relationship with Fritz became more and more formal. I was indulging in all the usual teenage hell-raising: cherry-bombing mailboxes, guzzling beer, running fast cars down country roads, that sort of thing. But Fritz enjoyed no similar period of adolescent wildness. The only pills he ever popped were vitamins, and I never saw his lips touch so much as a single can of beer. As a teenager, he was incredibly straight-laced, even puritanical. I never heard an obscene word pass his lips, not even when he was fully grown. He never talked about sex, either, even during the years when that subject has a tendency to chloroform the teenage brain.

During the Sixties, when the rest of us were smoking reefer and marching on Washington, Fritz cheered the faction that wanted to turn North Vietnam into a K mart parking lot. We were all dupes of the Red Menace, he insisted.

He was doing, all along, whatever he thought it would take to become just like his father, whether it was sharing Doctor Klenner's political values or his moral rigidity. That complemented Doctor Fred's feelings about Fritz. He wanted to be Fritz's closest friend and, in fact, ran interference to make sure that no one from outside the family could ever get close enough to be Fritz's buddy.

There was something hermetic about the family's arrangement, and in some ways it was a pretty nicely balanced equation: Doctor Klenner's smothering, possessive love for his son dovetailed neatly with Fritz's unquestioning worship of his father.

Internally, then, Fritz must have known a secure and self-contained world. It only started to appear nutty when you tried to reconcile it with outside realities. As long as Fritz could stay inside that world, or return to it periodically, his lid stayed screwed on to a certain extent. But when his father finally died, that special, safe wall died too.

CHAPTER EIGHT

Daddy's Boy

Fritz Klenner's biggest torment was that everybody expected him to follow in his father's footsteps — expected him not just to be a doctor, but also to be Fred's virtual reincarnation, to carry on in the same grandly eccentric style, maybe even to go beyond the medical frontiers so often crossed by his father and find some sort of vitamin cure for cancer.

Fritz's entire world was defined, bounded, and measured by his father, leaving the boy in a position of awe, fear, and utter helpless devotion to Doc Klenner. It was a heavy burden from an early age. He already wanted nothing in the world more than to be like his father; he didn't need to have everyone around him applying more and more pressure to force him into a groove to which he had already gravitated on his own.

Most fathers would have relished the sort of filial obedience Doc Klenner enjoyed from his only son. But Fritz's feelings went past devotion, into worship. And in his efforts to mold himself to the impossible template held up to him in the mirror, Fritz embraced every skewed idea and creed his father had dabbled in over the years: belief in the imminence of Armageddon, virulent hatred of Communists, blacks, and Jews, and a mystical, highly personalized, Roman Catholicism.

But whereas Doctor Fred had merely colored his life with these things, still functioning daily as a respected and popular physician, Fritz took everything and swallowed it whole — without a single recorded act of rebellion, defiance, self-assertion, or even, as far as family members can recall, very much argument. He then proceeded to carry these beliefs to a higher level of commitment than his father ever had. Doc Klenner had just spouted a lot of hot wind about Armageddon, but Fritz actually started drawing up scenarios for how he was going to convert that epic tragedy into a personal triumph.

Whereas Doc Klenner wore his eccentricities like a security blanket, his son donned them like a suit of glowing armor. Soon Fritz came to regard himself as a genuine *ubermensch* and began to couch his personal fantasies in terms of dogmatic, yet lofty, German mysticism.

Fritz's predisposition toward firearms, for instance, was inherited directly from his father. But where Doc Klenner saw guns as a manifestation of his right to bear arms, and mainly used them to have fun (banging away in the woods during their Bigfoot safaris), Fritz developed a genuine fetish for guns. He would caress his guns, inhale their oil-wood-leather-and-powder smells, savor their weight and balance, and study their lines with the same aroused intent of a girl-watcher contemplating a well-turned leg. He was excited by the latent potency that some people can feel locked up within the steel loins of a high-velocity weapon. A gun-fetish this strong can be every bit as obsessive as the classic sexual fixations on leather, rubber, or garter belts. The Freudian undercurrents are obvious: My gun's bigger than your gun.

As his fascination for weapons deepened, Fritz also became more interested in ancillary types of militaria. He gravitated, inevitably, toward the period and style which most openly acknowledged the inherent fetishism of uniforms: the black-leather and silver-skulled chic of the Third Reich. Not that he started wearing swastika arm bands to school or anything, but he did habitually deck himself out with bits of army surplus clothing, sheath knives, assorted pouches and scabbards, and camouflage-pattern clothing.

In his high school years, Fritz, although handsome, deliberately chose to be a loner. He paid little attention to girls; and the girls, thinking him decidedly odd, paid little attention to him. When he had free time, he didn't go out cruising with the other boys his age.

Instead, he just went down to his father's clinic and hung out, running errands, picking up pointers, already in training for his predestined role as "Young Doctor Klenner."

Adolescent or adult, bearded or clean-shaven, Fritz Klenner was a good-looking male, a classic specimen of wholesome teutonic virility. He had exceptional eyes, just like his father. Emotions coalesced in those eyes like weather fronts: warmth, concern, determination, arrogance, and a brooding, Heathcliffian aura of strength. He could look at someone and make his eyes reflect whatever emotion was required to mobilize his whole persona toward gaining an advantage over the other person. He undoubtedly accomplished a fair percentage of his many seductions — sexual, social, and psychological — by means of those eyes.

The beard he wore for much of his adult life was helpful, too. Luxuriant and thick, yet always immaculately clean and trimmed, it helped to offset his sole exaggerated feature: that large, patrician Klenner nose. Sometimes he would grow the beard, then shave it off after disappearing for a while from the life of one of his women. One did that sort of thing after a "mission," if one were engaged in top-secret enterprises.

The only photo of Fritz Klenner that does not reveal an almost palpable sense of purpose and confidence is his junior class picture from high school. This photograph seems to reveal the face of a confused and unhappy adolescent. It reveals something lonely and already lost in the eyes, something vulnerable and uncertain in the lines of his mouth — something that is so firm, so set, so controlled in every other photo.

The Reidsville public school system that Fritz attended became integrated in 1969, when he was a senior. Doctor Klenner was predictably disgusted by this turn of events, but said he wasn't surprised. Had he not mentioned, countless times, that public school integration (the first step toward mongrelizing the races) was a cherished element in the Commie-Zionist Master Plan? Just one more step on the road to Armageddon.

So, Doc's response to this threat was to yank Fritz out of the public school system altogether and enroll him at Woodward Academy, an expensive boarding school near Atlanta that offered a strong quasi-military program, a strict disciplinary code, and an ideological orientation which matched Doc Klenner's ideas of what was right and proper.

Under this new regimen, Fritz seemed to blossom. The sense of personal liberty, of being out from under all those stifling intimate expectations and obligations, must have been fairly intoxicating. He became much more active socially, and an eager participant in school affairs. His grades were superior, too, for the first and last time in his life. He graduated ninth in his class. He would never, however, become much of a scholar. Although he was an intense reader of certain kinds of books, and a natural, regurgitative sponge when it came to absorbing knowledge from his environment, his mind was not attuned to the classic disciplines of scholarship. Even as an adult, his handwriting revealed horrendous gaps in basic academic knowledge. His writing was burdened by the spelling and syntax of a sixth grader.

After graduating from Woodward Academy in 1970, Fritz entered the University of Mississippi at Jackson. He enrolled, to no one's surprise, as a pre-med student. And for the first time in his life, now that he was truly out of the nest, he fell in love with, or at least had a crush on, a young woman. He even, briefly, considered himself engaged. But the relationship did not last, and Fritz made sure, from that day forward, that every subsequent relationship he had with a woman was on his terms.

Sometime during his first year at Ole Miss, Fritz began to cast off his moorings. The games of adolescence slowly acquired greater meaning, and more consistent vividness, than the untidy demands of reality. His class attendance became erratic and his grades suffered accordingly. He spoke airily about entering Duke Medical School, seemingly unconcerned that a C-plus average was not likely to impress the admissions committee of that prestigious institution any more than Doctor Fred's vitamin cures for polio had impressed the medical establishment.

Fritz spent four years at Ole Miss, but never obtained a degree. Instead, he descended deeper into his fantasies. He sometimes wore concealed pistols to class, and he spoke darkly about his work as an undercover narcotics agent, about his paramilitary training sessions in secret camps out in the bayous, and about the dangerous missions he sometimes pursued. He became a 'Nam-dropper, alluding to Special Forces adventures out "in the bush," although both then and later he always clammed up about his supposed Vietnam experiences if there were any genuine veterans within earshot.

At first glance, it seems odd that he never made any serious attempt to join the armed forces. But the reality of military routine would have seemed too dull, too regimented, compared to the crypto-reality he was busily constructing for himself. And as for joining one of the elite fighting units such as the Marines, the U.S. Army Special Forces, or the Navy's SEAL teams — where there was a chance of real action even in peacetime — well, what Fritz wanted to do was have *fun* with this stuff, not put himself through the months and months of training-camp hell required to qualify for such an outfit.

According to the plan Doc Klenner had for his son, Fritz would sail through his pre-med years at Ole Miss, then head straight for Daddy's alma mater, Duke Medical School. But at the end of his four years at Mississippi, Fritz was shy the number of credits needed for graduation. Dutifully, he went to summer school in 1974; but when autumn came, he was still short the required credits.

Fritz told his father he was taking a correspondence course to make up what he lacked, and assured him that he would indeed obtain his diploma, in the mail, after the university's "Christmas commencement."

When the summer of 1975 arrived and the "Christmas diploma" still hadn't, Doctor Klenner contacted the university and learned the truth: Fritz still lacked the credits he needed to graduate and, no, the school had no such thing as a Christmas commencement.

Fritz explained to his father that this failure was the result of machinations by enemies in the school administration and faculty who had been sabotaging his work for a long time. He promised his father it would be taken care of. But it never was, and Fritz never received his diploma from Mississippi.

The whole business was more than a little bit curious. On the surface, Fritz wanted nothing more in the world than to go to Duke and become a doctor, just as his father had done. But during his last two years at Ole Miss, he probably started to realize that passing through Duke Medical School was going to be the intellectual equivalent of qualifying for the Green Berets. By that time, he must have known something of the truth about his own limitations as a scholar. Besides, his fantasy-life as Young Doctor Klenner was already too rich for him to risk any prolonged and abrasive contact with med school realities.

On the other hand, it's also possible that this refusal to buckle down and get those last few credits might have been Fritz Klenner's one and only gesture of youthful rebellion against his father and family. If so, it manifested itself in such a twisted and sublimated way that one doubts Fritz was able to diagnose it for what it was.

CHAPTER NINE

Bringing Up Susie

On Christmas Eve, 1947, Doctor Frederick Klenner delivered Susie Newsom, the first child of Robert Jr. and Florence Sharp Newsom. Her only sibling, Robert Newsom III, was born December 19, 1949.

Susie was named after her famous aunt, Florence's older sister, North Carolina Supreme Court Justice Susie Sharp. As soon as little Susie could talk, she started calling her namesake "Aunt Su-Su." As often happens with such nicknames, the rest of the family picked it up.

At that time, the Newsoms were living outside Winston-Salem near the old Moravian community of Bethabara. Their house, a ranch-style dwelling of solid middle-class appointments, was situated on a pleasantly landscaped rural site, complete with numerous trees, a pond, riding paths, and lots of animals. Not far away, on Valley Road in Old Town, was the home of Susie's grandparents, Hattie and Robert Newsom Sr. As Susie grew up, she took particular pleasure in visiting her "Nana" and "Paw Paw."

Soon after Susie's birth, Doctor Klenner told her parents that their newborn child had a "heart murmur." He warned that she should not be allowed to cry. Obviously, this doctor's order was not only impossible to fulfill, but also made Bob and Florence's first year with Susie unnaturally tense and edgy.

The next time Susie's path crossed the Klenners' was when she turned six, during the polio years in America. Susie had been to a birthday party with a girl who a short time later came down with the dreaded disease. Susie's parents took her to Doctor Klenner, who confirmed that Susie had indeed contracted polio. He immediately began treating her with enormous, and rather painful, injections of vitamin C. Since Susie never became paralyzed, or suffered any other polio symptoms, for that matter, her parents concluded that Doctor Klenner's unorthodox treatment had worked.

Susie Newsom grew up to be vivacious and attractive, with a pretty, round face, vital brown eyes, a mouth that carried just a hint of the sensual, and a slim, tennis-court figure. She achieved, and clearly enjoyed, a certain degree of popularity even while quite young — she was chosen as Queen of the May while still in kindergarten. But there was a shyness coupled with a sense of social station that sometimes made her appear reserved, even standoffish, by the time she reached senior high school.

Still, as a member of a prominent, widely respected family, Susie had security and self-esteem. If her family was special, so was she; never mind what the other kids thought. The world of adulthood promised to be a pleasant environment, thanks to the prominence Susie's social position would bring her.

Her appreciation of the perks of social position was keen, but ambivalent. As a teenager, she became infatuated with the British royal family. Each year, on the Queen's birthday, she decorated her room with bunting, Union Jacks, and pin-ups of the various royals. On the other hand, when it was pointed out to her that she was entitled to a place on the statewide debutante list, she refused to consider it, saying that it was vulgar, ostentatious, and quite beneath her.

She had an excellent academic record in high school, graduating with honors from North Forsyth High in 1964. She enrolled in Queens College in Charlotte, but grew dissatisfied and transferred to Wake Forest University in Winston-Salem after her sophomore year.

It was at Wake Forest that she met her future husband, Tom Lynch, a tall, conventionally handsome blond athlete with a good smile and a talent on the basketball court that stopped just short of the first rank. The relationship between Susie and Tom was, for all intents and purposes, an ordinary campus romance, except for one point that seemed minor at the time: Susie was two years older than Tom. This was not significant to Tom Lynch while they were dating; in fact, it implied a subtle flattery which could only have pleased him. But the age difference was a factor that would later give Susie a sense of superiority.

By Tom's junior year at Wake Forest, he and Susie were seriously planning marriage. Everything was going smoothly until Tom brought Susie home to Kentucky to meet his mother, Delores Lynch. Susie and Delores disliked each other instantly and profoundly. Susie thought Delores was a witch. And Delores sensed something about Susie that made her uneasy; perhaps a latent arrogance raised her motherly hackles. Susie didn't have to sniff this out, either: Delores had never been one to hide her feelings. And Susie quite naturally disliked anyone who disliked her. Tom was smitten with Susie, however, and he thought the tension between the two women would diminish as they got to know one another. Instead, the more they saw of each other, the faster their mutual dislike evolved into detestation.

Susie Newsom married Tom Lynch at St. Paul's Episcopal Church in Winston-Salem on June 6, 1970. The tension between Susie and Delores was thick and unpleasant. The wedding was one of the bigger social events of the season, but beneath the outward ceremonies there was plenty of turmoil: Susie sniping at Delores, Delores huffing back at Susie, Susie telling Tom's sister, Jane Lynch, that her dress was tacky, that sort of thing.

There was no time for a honeymoon. Tom was on a tight schedule, having been accepted at dental school at the University of Kentucky in Lexington. Delores did her mother-in-law's duty and helped the newlyweds find an apartment near the campus. Susie landed a good-paying job with a local company. Since Tom's family was paying for his educational expenses, the young couple was able to live quite decently, although their conflicting personal schedules kept them on separate tracks most of the time.

The Lynch family lived only 85 miles away, yet only once, during the more than three years that Tom and Susie lived in Lexington, did they drive as a couple to the Lynch home. That was on Thanksgiving Day, 1970. Otherwise, contact between Susie and Delores was minimal. If they spoke, it was on the telephone, and then only to transact business, not make chit-chat.

Tom had decided that a hitch in the Navy would be good experience before setting up a private dental practice. He was commissioned as a Navy dentist in 1974 and assigned to Parris Island. He and Susie set up their private housekeeping at nearby Beaufort, South Carolina. By all accounts, the ensuing two-year period seems to have been the happiest of the entire marriage. Tom's career was on track and Susie felt right at home in Beaufort, with its elegant architecture, orderly and stratified society, Old South traditions, and WASP aristocracy.

Their first child, John, was born August 30, 1974, at the base hospital where Tom worked. The second boy, Jim, was born on March 26, 1976.

When John was born, Delores Lynch was naturally excited about the arrival of her first grandchild. She visited Beaufort to get acquainted with the baby, but the visit was a disaster. Although Susie's house had a perfectly suitable guest room, Susie insisted that Delores stay at a motel. Furthermore, she demanded that Delores actually make an appointment to see her grandchild.

When Tom was discharged from the Navy in 1976, he decided to set up his practice somewhere out west. He had always felt the appeal of a desert landscape, and he liked wide horizons. He heard about a new practice opening up in Albuquerque, New Mexico, checked it out, and very much liked what he saw.

Susie didn't. She found New Mexico loathsome. When they moved there later in 1976, an initial period of diffidence gave way to vocal complaint. Susie didn't like it there and didn't mind saying so to anyone who'd listen. Albuquerque was the pits, she said. No culture; too many Mexicans and Indians; no classical music closer than Santa Fe. And she hated the desert. She hated, most of all, the fact that out there, in that raw and uncultured landscape, nobody knew who she was or gave a damn if her aunt was on the Supreme Court of North Carolina and had appeared on the cover of *Time*.

Still, for the first months they lived in New Mexico, she went dutifully through the motions of helping Tom get established. But then her friends noticed that, after a year or so of generalized complaining about the area, she seemed to focus on specific complaints against her husband. Tom was basically nothing but a jock, she said. And his mother, Delores, was an utter bitch. When Delores sent packages to the grandchildren, Susie threw them away unopened.

By the start of Tom and Susie's third year in Albuquerque, friends who once felt welcome in the Lynch home had stopped coming by. Susie's incessant carping and bad-mouthing had become too unpleasant.

Aside from the personal disillusionments of the marriage, the root of her discontent was probably the simple fact that the Sharp/Newsom name meant nothing in New Mexico. Stripped of her social identity for the first time in her life, Susie felt rootless, unfocused, angry. She bored their new friends with her constant bragging about her uncle, "the world-famous Doctor Klenner," and her aunt, the chief justice.

She fought with Tom a great deal, and worse, began to take out some of her hostilities on the two boys. They were old enough now to start asserting their own identities, and that seemed to rub her raw on certain days. Her relationship with her sons was losing its balance, with Susie alternately smothering them with overprotection and then slapping them around. In the spring of 1979, she smacked little Jim so hard that he ended up in the hospital with a concussion.

Sometime during the spring of 1978, Susie began to break away. She took a job of her own and did well at it. In her youth, she had a passionate interest in the Orient, an interest which now returned with new enthusiasm. She began to study Mandarin Chinese.

The marriage finally ruptured in the spring of 1979, after a series of escalating marital conflicts. Susie told neighbors who were still speaking to her that she was taking the boys back to North Carolina to visit their grandfather, Paw Paw Newsom, who was in declining health. But when she loaded the boys into the family Audi that July, it must have been clear to everybody who knew her that she was making a permanent break from her marriage with Tom. She was fleeing back to a place where the fame of her namesake, of Chief Justice Susie Sharp, would help her command the respect to which she felt entitled.

Some Things About Susie That Didn't Make the Papers

My sister Susie and I grew up in one of the most idyllic pastoral environments you could imagine: this lovely little farm up in rural Forsyth County. We had a pond to splash in, plenty of room to roam around in, and ponies and lots of other animals.

My sister had this marvelously gentle touch with animals. Dogs obeyed her without hesitation. The ponies never bit her, never balked, never threw her. She had the potential to be a superb horse-woman.

After all the murders, some of the newspaper stories about Susie made her out to be some kind of spoiled WASP princess who expected everybody to wait on her hand and foot, an *enfant terrible* who threw tantrums from the day she was born. That's neither fair nor accurate.

There was the story, for example, that recounted how she had such wild fits of temper as a child that my parents had to throw her into tubs full of ice water to calm her down. Sounds pretty psychotic, doesn't it? In fact, what was happening was nothing more than what happens with many kids when they reach the Terrible Twos — they get so wound up that they get beside themselves and can't stop crying. Most parents have to deal with such episodes every now and then during that period of a child's development. Susie's pediatrician suggested that a quick dunk in cold water was usually a good way to snap a child out of these episodes when they were otherwise beyond consolation. My mother and father tried it a few times and it worked. Like every other normal infant, she grew out of that stage, and that was the end of it. It was not as though they had to keep a tub full of ice water handy at all times in case Susie suddenly started running amok. It was no big deal and it only happened a few times.

Her hunger for culture was not superficial, but a very important part of her makeup. She had a deep appreciation for, and a better than fair knowledge of, classical music, dance, and drama. She was a passionate historian, too, and read extensively. Her interest in the Orient, in fact, probably derives from her infatuation with the novels of Pearl Buck and the historical narratives of Barbara Tuchman.

My dad raised us on the farm, even though we were very middle-class people, because he wanted us to avoid contact with what he perceived as the dangers and temptations of growing up in the big city. But it didn't quite work out that way. Both Susie and I were always acutely conscious of how different we were from our rural neighbors. I coped with that by learning how to talk like a redneck and drink Pabst Blue Ribbon. Susie coped with it by withdrawing, by turning her sense of isolation into a feeling of specialness and privilege.

But Susie was not the arrogant, imperious woman often depicted later in the newspapers. She was not motivated by anything as simple and crass as elitism. She merely had a profound sense of not belonging, and when she was a teenager the other kids usually interpreted that kind of insecurity as haughtiness.

One of the main reasons she left Queens College in Charlotte and transferred to Wake Forest University in Winston-Salem was her conviction that Queens was too much of a country club, that all the little debs who went there thought themselves too special for words. She used to complain that the only thing that seemed important to those girls was who had the latest Ship 'n' Shore blouse or Villager dress.

During the turmoil of the Sixties, Susie stayed on the sidelines. She was politically very conservative, and morally she was something of a Calvinist, though how she came by that rigid outlook remains a mystery to me to this day.

My sister's fatal character flaw, then, was something more subtle than any of those attributed to her in the newspaper accounts. Much more subtle, and far more mysterious.

It was a perception of morality, of God if you like, that reinforced her sense of isolation, but certainly did not spring from it. It certainly didn't come from the Episcopal church our family attended; I doubt if there's ever been a real get-down fire-and-brimstone type of sermon preached within its walls. Everybody was far too genteel for that sort of carrying-on.

Susie's unyielding attitude toward life came from her belief that there was such a thing as an irredeemable mistake — that you could do something wrong and there was no way you could ever put it right. On the positive side, this made her a very rule-oriented and obedient child. I doubt if she ever once knowingly disobeyed a parental order. On the negative side, she had this propensity for sudden, fierce, uncompromising anger. One wrong move, one uncalled-for remark, and she crossed you off her list. Forever.

I remember, for example, a party during which one of my father's friends started teasing Susie, telling her that she was just too pretty to really be her father's child, that she must have been conceived while he was away in the Merchant Marine. At worst, it was a somewhat tasteless bit of ribbing, but not the sort of thing you would carry a grudge about to the grave, especially if the guy doing the joking had sipped a highball or two. But Susie just got up, gave him this icy glance, walked out of the room, and never spoke to him again. Three or four years later, when Mom and Dad wanted to include him on the list of people invited to Susie's wedding, she struck his name from the list.

There's another clue, perhaps, in the way Susie responded to certain Bible stories when she was young. She had a lot of trouble with some Sunday school classes about the parables. The prodigal son, the woman taken in adultery, the woman at the well, the parable of the sheep and the goats — she just didn't buy any of them. She would not allow herself to be convinced that Jesus actually promulgated those teachings.

The common thread running through all those stories that she couldn't accept is the concept of forgiveness. Susie's God was a judgmental God, a God of vengeance. To her way of thinking, there were strict account books being kept in heaven, and if you couldn't produce your receipts, you were in for it. You paid for what you did wrong. Period.

At the same time, she saw herself as always being right with that God. She had never done anything wrong; only other people around her had. And God was someday going to get them for it.

If you start out in life with that attitude, and then add to it all the ordinary unhappy things that just happen to people in their adulthood — marriages that fail, the frustrations and disappointments of parenthood, the feeling that life is just not keeping the promises it once made to you — then you can easily develop a feeling that other folks' misdeeds are the cause of it all.

You can see the same syndrome, writ large, in the concepts behind some of the extreme survivalist groups that Fritz Klenner sympathized with. Look at those guys in the Posse Comitatus movement — they believe there is some vast Jewish-Communist cabal of bankers and money-changers in the Eastern big cities who are directly responsible for some poor guy in South Dakota losing the family farm. The Rothschilds and the Rockefellers and the Arabs are all conspiring to jack up the price of oil and make it impossible for the little guy to buy fertilizer and fuel for his tractors.

For a lot of people, it's easier to swallow that version of things than it is to accept the truth, which may be that the farm went under due to bad lending practices, or because the farmer over-borrowed, or because that way of life is historically doomed and that's just tough. But the victim is hurt to the bone, and he feels in his gut there has to be somebody out there who is responsible. It cannot, after all, be the victim himself who bears any responsibility; it is always easier to accept a catastrophe by rationalizing that you would have been powerless to prevent it anyway.

It was the same with Susie. She couldn't see herself as being wrong because, in her mind, that led to terrible, irredeemable consequences.

When you reach the stage of starting to deny external reality, as well as personal responsibility for screwing up, then you become a sitting duck for somebody like Charles Manson or the Reverend Moon or Lyndon LaRouche...or Fritz Klenner.

Some Things About Me That Did Make the Papers

At about the same time Susie's marriage to Tom Lynch was disintegrating in New Mexico, in the late 1970s, I was enduring a roughly analogous watershed in my own life. Both of us reached our respective crises by following the same basic blueprint for life, one we had developed out of the family attitudes that had shaped our formative years. Our courses were, in a sense, parallel, up to the time when we each fell into the abyss. I responded in a certain way, recovered, and went on to a richer and more productive life. Susie reacted in a different way and went into a downward spiral that resulted in tragedy.

One of the things I think I've learned is that a person's outlook as he or she matures may not be shaped so much by what your family actually does or says, but on how the family was perceived when you were young.

This extended family of ours, the Newsoms and the Sharps, despite all the individual achievement, was, in some ways, a "hurting" family. Along with the accomplishments people pointed to, there was an extraordinary degree of denial, of stuffing the problems somewhere to get them out of sight. For instance, look at how the family responded to the phenomenon of Doc Klenner. To the outside world, we spoke only about the wealthy and powerful people who came all the way to Reidsville for treatment, about his being mentioned by Linus Pauling, about his medical degree from Duke, and about his medical genius. We never mentioned that he stalked Bigfoot on the family farm or practiced exorcisms.

We grew up with an expectation of unblemished success. This is not to say that our parents tried to imprint that expectation on our minds from infancy. It's just that the whole family generated a certain pervasive attitude that evolved into the assumption of success in life. You can give children expectations indirectly by filling their ears with family lore in which failure is ignored, in which no one ever speaks about hardships endured with dignity or mistakes that were made and lived down by men and women who were able to learn from them. In our family, we had no tales about people who had earned forgiveness and started their lives anew. Those things seemed to us to be part of other peoples' stories, not our own. Eventually, both Susie and I started to see ourselves as needing to be perfect, or at least needing to appear that way.

There's a family anecdote that illustrates how this peculiar philosophy worked among us. When we were cleaning out my mother's personal effects after her death, we discovered a lovely letter written to her by Justice Susie Sharp, written at a time when my mother was very depressed because my dad had lost his job with Lorillard. In the letter, Justice Sharp told about the time when Grandfather Sharp had gone into the sawmill business up in Virginia with a hard-drinking relative. They lost their shirts. Now, Justice Sharp must have been a very small girl when that business went into receivership, but she still remembered vividly the day when the appraisers came to take away all their personal property to pay the creditors. In particular, she remembered the tremendous gentle dignity with which her mother bore the hardship as the family was completely wiped out. They had to start life all over again.

Grandfather Sharp later became a respected lawyer, a legislator, and a highly regarded citizen. The incredible thing is that my mother never had even heard of that episode about her own mother and father until Justice Sharp wrote her about it, when my mother was in her fifties. That part of Grandpa Sharp's story was swept under the rug by everyone, by tacit agreement, as if it were something dark and shameful.

It's a wonderful story, not a sad one, about hard times borne with dignity and courage, and about rising above defeat. It is every bit as important that Grandpa Sharp suffered that failure as it is that he served in the state legislature. But *nobody* in the family even mentioned that episode for almost half a century. Tragedies as well as triumphs are a part of every family's heritage. But in our family, the custom was to deny that the tragedies and failures had ever occurred. And that led to a set of very unrealistic expectations.

So my sister Susie and I grew up along two different but parallel routes. She had a genuine, authentic expectation of perfection. After all, look how many other family members had achieved such states of grace. No disgraces, no failures, no blemishes in their past histories.

My approach to life started from the same place but followed a slightly different route: I believed that all that really mattered was the appearance of complete success. It seemed perfectly okay to me, when I got to college, to party all semester and be drunk half the time, just as long as I could buckle down with a supply of amphetamines when exam time rolled around. As long as I got As and Bs, it didn't matter much what was going on between report cards.

The same pattern carried over into my early career as an attorney. As long as it looked good and sounded good, things were going according to the traditional family program and all was right with my world. I rode the drugs all the way through college. By my senior year, I was shooting up meth crystals, because my tolerance had outgrown mere pills. When I went out into the legal world, I simply exchanged one dependency for another. I saw all these successful lawyers around me who drank a lot, and since drinking seemed acceptable, it replaced the speed.

I soon left North Carolina and accepted a job as a corporate lawyer for an oil company in Houston. I needed the higher salary, because I was drinking away so much of my money and could no longer handle my financial affairs responsibly. The oil company handed me a dream situation: an unlimited expense account and the chance to travel a lot. If you want to kill an alcoholic with kindness, just set him up with an expense account and a lot of time on airplanes. Whatever self-control I still had disappeared rapidly.

Fortunately, my boss in Houston had some insight into alcoholism and maneuvered me into a position where I could no longer escape the realization that I was doing a lousy job as a lawyer and that my drinking was the reason. I still tried to keep up those precious outward appearances of success, but I was falling apart inside.

The turning point, the place where I bottomed out, was when I realized it was not the end of the world, nor necessarily the end of Bob Newsom III, if I admitted to myself and to the world that I had an illness. To accept the fact that it just happens. People get sick, people make mistakes, people sometimes land in jail. Life goes on, *if* you let it.

It was long and painful process, but I came to understand that even the appearance of perfection is not an acceptable goal for human beings. It is *all right* to accept your mistakes. It is okay not to be perfect. It is even okay not to pretend to be perfect.

I left the practice of law. It was announced in the bar association journal that I had gone on "inactive status," a euphemism that fooled nobody. In truth, if I had not done this on my own, I would have been disbarred. Things had gotten that bad. I went to work as a counselor for the Guilford County Alcoholism Services.

Working in that treatment center taught me a lot. I was able to achieve a certain detachment from my own situation and to view my whole life in a new perspective. In 1984, I became court counselor for the Alcoholism Services. My job was to go through the prison system and try to identify people who were caught in that system by their drinking, and to try to find help for them.

It was necessary for me to tell some of those people that I was a lawyer on inactive status because until recently I had been a drunken incompetent. And I got a big surprise: I did not suffer any rejection or stigma. I found instead a remarkable degree of acceptance and good will. The whole experience sealed my belief that all the world can realistically expect of you is that you do the best you can at that particular moment. I also came to believe that the people who go bust are also the people who learn the most from rising above it.

Susie, as she grew into adulthood, was afflicted with a mirror image of my syndrome. I was dedicated to appearing perfect, but Susie took it one step further. She actually believed she *had* to be perfect, and so did everyone else in her life. To her, the consequences of imperfection were dreadful and unacceptable. So when things went wrong, she concluded that it just had to be someone else's fault.

She looked at the family's attitude and drew the conclusion: Hey, we don't have divorces in this family, we don't live in places like Albuquerque, we don't fail in our undertakings. Neither God nor the family would tolerate it.

I tried to discuss some of these things a few times with my sister. This new awareness, this new awakening, as I had come to think of it, was utterly incomprehensible to her. I think her mind just stopped right at the point where my name appeared in the bar association journal under the euphemistic "inactive status" label. To her, my life ceased at that label, with its implications of shame and failure. Nothing moved beyond that. She never understood that it had been a point of departure for me, that I had accepted all the bad things I'd done, all the failures of will and courage, and was using them as a foundation to build on. She saw me as permanently branded. I was so happy that I had learned how to look back on all that as history, but Susie was utterly unable to see the total process. She could only focus on that downward curve away from the family ideal of unblemished success.

You cannot measure your self-worth by the yardstick of your past actions. You have to measure it by what you're doing right this minute, and you have to use that as your basis for relating to the world around you.

Susie needed to accept that her marriage had not worked out, and that it didn't matter a bit, in the long run, who had been at fault. She needed to accept that it didn't *matter* any more that her plans for a perfect life didn't pan out, and it didn't even matter *why*, really. It isn't possible to go through life without making mistakes, but that concept had never been part of Susie's thought processes. When some big mistakes happened, she just ran into a brick wall. From about 1981 onward, I started to see life as an organic, evolving process. Susie saw it as a monolith, a succession of absolute, black-or-white states of being.

By the time I tried to talk to my sister, it was too late for Susie to reorder her way of thinking. In her mind, she had *not* made a mistake. Rather, she had been wronged and cheated out of her perfect-life scenario. The normal evolution of her life ground to a halt at that point, while she grew angrier and angrier and wondered how to make somebody pay for it. That's why it was so easy for her to accept some of the rationalizations offered to her by Fritz Klenner.

I can't help but wonder what might have happened if the timing had been different. Perhaps if I had gone all the way through my own crisis before her problems with Fritz came to my attention, I could have been more effective in helping her. But her downward spiral coincided with my first, faltering steps back from my own abyss, and my only real priority at the time was to get myself straightened out.

Susie, too, had the opportunity to learn from the bad things that had happened to her, but she rejected even the possibility. She could not grow beyond the bitterness, the anger, the sense of having been cheated out of something to which she had a right.

Today, as a public defender, I handle a lot of people who are guilty. No question about it: They did exactly what the police said they did, and maybe a lot more besides. But you know something? I really *like* most of my clients. They're people who have made some serious mistakes and they owe society (and maybe some individuals) a certain amount of recompense, but they are not evil or worthless or irredeemable. There is goodness in all of them, except for the occasional outright sociopath. As I write this, I have about 140 cases sitting on my desk, and out of that number, there are maybe only ten people whom I simply cannot abide. The rest are good people who've screwed up and are trying to put it behind them.

But my sister could never see things that way.

CHAPTER TWELVE

There and Back Again

Once Susie Newsom Lynch was settled back in her familiar hometown area of Winston-Salem, she sought legal help and arranged for a separation agreement from Tom Lynch. It took effect in September 1979. By this time, Susie had learned that Tom was seeking solace in the company of his dental assistant, a woman whom he would later marry. Although Susie had lacked any marital interest in Tom for some time, she was still outraged when she found out and railed bitterly against his "immorality" and "unfitness."

While Susie was trying to untangle herself from the past, she was also making plans for a new start. She decided to turn her lifelong infatuation with things Oriental into a career. She applied to and was accepted by the University of Taiwan's Mandarin language school. She was also able to secure a position teaching English at the College of Chinese Culture there.

There was nothing irrational or half-baked about this decision. It's hard, in fact, to perceive it as anything other than a gutsy, even bold, attempt by an embittered young woman to pick up the pieces of her life by striking off in a totally new direction.

Tom Lynch hated the idea of Susie taking their two boys off to the Far East, of course, and Susie's own family thought the whole thing was a bit off the wall, too. Nevertheless, she was clearly determined to go, and the Newsoms eventually decided that such a total break with the past might be therapeutic for their daughter. Susie departed for the Orient on December 28, 1979, planning to stay for a year.

The exotic East, she soon discovered, was a lot better in her dreams than in reality. She loathed what she perceived as her squalid living conditions, although, by Taiwanese standards, she was living in decidedly middle-class comfort. Her neighborhood was crowded with people — foreigners! — and with smells and debris and all the usual sorts of local color that don't make the travel brochures. It was here that Susie developed a phobia about germs — a phobia that Fritz Klenner would later play on with consummate virtuosity. The very idea of germs was something that she would associate, for the rest of her life, with the teeming, yeasty conditions of life on Taiwan.

It only took about six weeks for Susie to suffer one of the biggest disillusionments of her life. The promised land she had sought in the Orient turned out to be just as complicated and compromised as the promised land of being married to a successful dentist in America. The boys' health deteriorated under the conditions of their new environment and diet. At one point, little Jim had to be hospitalized, a setback which took a big bite out of Susie's modest savings. On top of this, she was compelled to maintain a frantic academic schedule. Then word came that her beloved grandfather, Paw Paw Newsom, had died.

To her credit, she kept plugging away, determined to stay at least long enough to finish some research projects she had started. However, her six-month tourist visa was about to expire and she was having trouble getting an extension. Aunt Susie Sharp intervened by asking for help from North Carolina Senator Jesse Helms. He in turn leaned on the right desks in the Taiwanese bureaucracy, and the visa problem was taken care of.

Even so, Susie left Taiwan in June 1980, six months earlier than planned. Delores Lynch met her and the boys at O'Hare International Airport in Chicago, and it was perhaps the only moment in their bristly relationship when Susie treated her mother-in-law with anything approaching genuine warmth — a measure of how beaten down she was by the whole wretched experience.

The only positive aspect of it all for Susie was her new sense of closeness to the boys. They had shared so much together in Taiwan, and their relationship had been such an anchor for her, that she now felt an almost hysterically intense sense of bonding with them.

A few months after Susie had returned from the Orient, she began telling friends that she had been stalked by "agents" in Taiwan, that her mail had been intercepted and steamed open, and that she had "escaped" from that country only after high-level intervention by Senator Jesse Helms, who had been forced to call in some heavy-duty favors from the Nationalist government to get her out of danger. All of this would have been very surprising news indeed to any of her Taiwanese friends, not to mention Senator Helms, who had probably taken care of the visa business with one or two friendly phone calls via an aide.

Susie had always expressed forceful opinions, but friends who heard her ranting in this vein started to wonder where she was getting all these queer ideas. It was almost as if someone were putting them into her mind.

CHAPTER THIRTEEN

The Worst Thing in the World

When Fritz Klenner suddenly announced, late in 1976, that he had been accepted at Duke Medical School — even though he still hadn't received his undergraduate degree from Mississippi — Doctor Klenner didn't even blink. Instead, he went out and bought his son a BMW 320 so Fritz could drive to med school in proper style. Every Monday morning, Fritz would roar off to Durham, where he kept an apartment on LaSalle Street. Every Friday night he returned to Reidsville, full of boastful stories about his academic progress. "Young Doctor Klenner," some of ol' Doc Fred's patients started calling him.

No one really knows just what Fritz did with all of his free time during the week when he was supposedly attending Duke Medical School. One of his major activities, though, was befriending some of the Raleigh-Hillsborough area paramilitary groups. He spent a lot of his days and nights hanging around the homes and shops of other young men who shared both his right-wing politics and his passion for guns.

Fritz usually arrived in a white lab coat with a stethoscope dangling from one pocket, toting an old-fashioned doctor's bag crammed with instruments, drugs, syringes, and huge supplies of vitamins. The vitamins he gobbled by the fistful, as though they were M & M candies. He also forced them on anyone else who would stand for it. As time went on, there were fewer and fewer takers.

He was involved in vital hush-hush research with his eminent father, he said. Sometimes it was atomic energy; other times it was bacteriological warfare, contract work for The Company (as insiders invariably referred to the Central Intelligence Agency). Enemy agents had tried to assassinate Doctor Klenner, but he, Fritz (proudly displaying some not-very-serious scratches), had foiled their plots and saved his father's life.

In his hip pocket, Fritz carried scraps of paper covered with mystic-religious writings that made no sense to anyone he showed them to. He also showed off some sinister, threatening letters from unnamed enemies. Since Fritz's handwriting was quite distinctive — with its fat, infantile letters, as well as his habitual misspellings of certain common words — it didn't take long to figure out that Fritz was actually mailing these dire missives to himself.

In time, the gun enthusiasts Fritz hung out with realized that he was a can or two shy of a six-pack. Behind his back, they started calling him Doctor Crazy.

To most of those who knew him in those days, he often seemed to be drowning in suppressed rage. Most of the time it was directed against the usual scapegoats: Commies, Jews, queers, and niggers. But sometimes it was directed at women. And a whole lot of the time, it was directed at his mother's family, the Sharps. How he despised them, with their noses in the air, always looking down at the Klenners, always making fun of Doctor Fred and his strange ways. More than once, he rambled on about how much fun it would be to rub their noses in the dirt.

Well, (he often concluded his diatribes on a philosophical note), that stuff was all going to be okay soon. Real soon, if he had read the omens correctly. The collapse of civilization was imminent. Unlike his other stories, this talk of the apocalypse *did* go over well with the people Fritz hung around with. The fantasy-fulfillment scenarios opened up by Doomsday were infinite in their variety, and many a rhapsodic hour was passed by groups of good ol' boys sitting around drinking beer, running wire brushes through the barrels of their AR-15s, and deciding who they would shoot first as soon as it was okay to do it.

For most of them, it was just good ol' boy bull. It was apparent to his listeners, though, that Fritz took it more seriously. When contradictions start to pile up (and by 1980, they were piling up fast for Fritz Klenner), and when mutually incompatible demands create stresses which cannot be internally resolved, some people turn to the comfort of a crisis philosophy: the idea that some vast, external disaster will reshuffle the deck, will break the rules which now confine and restrict, will open new possibilities and freedom of action where now there are only dead ends and impotent rage.

How Fritz hungered for that Judgment Day! He was prepared. He was ready. He was utterly convinced that he would come out on the other side of the holocaust not merely a survivor, but as one of the elite who would control whatever was left.

Some idea of what Fritz Klenner's Fourth Reich might have been like can be surmised from a remark made to one of his survivalist buddies in 1980: "If things really get bad," he said, "you can always take something worthless, like people, and make something valuable out of the raw materials, like fertilizer."

While these delicate sentiments were maturing in his brain and vengeful dreams about the Sharp family were (somewhat) helping to relax him, Fritz was still, quite successfully, leading an incredible double life. Every weekend he drove his BMW back to Reidsville from Durham and discussed, in great technical detail, the courseload of a medical student at Duke. If you took Fritz's word for it, everything was going quite well.

His new girlfriend Ruth, the daughter of a patient at his father's clinic, did take Fritz's word for it. They had been dating with increasing seriousness for about a year. By Christmas, they had reached the stage of planning a wedding. However, not long before the appointed marriage date, Fritz broke off the engagement in his own peculiar way. He told Ruth that he had stomach cancer.

Months later, in 1978, he announced himself cured, thanks to Doctor Klenner's unorthodox treatments. Now that he was well again,

Fritz renewed his nuptial agreement with Ruth. They were married two days before Christmas, 1978, at a Catholic church in Greensboro. The couple set up housekeeping in an apartment in Reidsville, not far from Doctor Klenner's clinic. But Fritz was still spending Monday through Friday in Durham. Attending classes at Duke, he maintained.

One of the things he was actually doing, from late 1980 onward, was engaging in the first of a series of at least five love affairs with older, emotionally troubled women. Three of those women had young sons. In these relationships, Fritz proved to be a consummate manipulator. He was, at first, a patient and sympathetic listener. He psyched people out quickly that way, learning where all of their weaknesses were, then closing in and taking over their lives. It was always subtle at first. He zeroed in on the needs and weaknesses of the people he sought to control, and then played to their vulnerabilities with what can only be described as a kind of genius.

One way he got to these women was by taking lots of time to befriend their sons. He took time to appear interested in them, to gain their confidence, to dazzle them by talking all sorts of he-man jive.

It's possible that his interest in young boys was sincere and that there were homoerotic and pedophiliac overtones that may or may not have been subconscious. Whether he ever acted out those impulses, if they were present at all, is not known and probably never will be.

By 1980, Fritz was discovering that reality cannot be shaped to one's personal needs. But some people can be molded into shapes that satisfy the needs of a dominant personality. Fritz had charisma, and he had charm that could be turned on and off at will. He had a remarkably keen ability, as do many sociopaths, to simulate whatever emotional response was required in a given situation to give himself a subtle edge.

The first such woman with whom he had an affair not only severed all ties with her husband and family, but also continued to believe Fritz's promises of marriage and fidelity even after learning that he already had a wife back in Reidsville. She finally began to back out of the relationship when she realized not only that Fritz was a habitual and extravagant liar, but also that no woman's love, not hers, not Ruth's, not anybody's, mattered to Fritz in any deep, abiding sense. The only thing on earth that did seem to matter to him was his father's opinion.

And even that was now in jeopardy, as the medical school scam, at long last, began to unravel. It appears that the first thread to come loose was Fritz's incompetence as a fledgling physician. A survivalist pal's wife had sought treatment from Fritz, and whatever he had done had made her thoroughly ill.

Another thing he had done was seduce her, and when that became known, Fritz's former buddy got together with some of the other folks who had been growing uneasy about Doctor Crazy, and they held discussions about having him committed. When they learned there was no legal chance of locking him away, they did something quite unusual for right-wing extremists: they ratted on him to the State Bureau of Investigation (SBI). They provided the SBI with a complete description of Fritz's behavior, including the fact that he was freely dispensing drugs, practicing medicine without a license, and trafficking in automatic weapons. Their description (from what is known about it — the file has never been made public by the SBI) certainly backed up their claim that Fritz Klenner should be considered a dangerous and heavily armed psychopath.

It is not unreasonable to wonder why, therefore, the SBI never acted on this information. The SBI has never explained, other than to remark that it cannot be expected to act on every report it gets about a potentially violent oddball.

Starting in the spring of 1981, the unravelling of Fritz's elaborately constructed life escalated sharply. First, Ruth discovered that Fritz was having an affair. At the same time came the possibly even more shattering discovery that he was not, and never had been, enrolled at Duke Medical School. Ruth left him, taking the BMW. She got in touch with Fritz's girlfriend in Durham, and together they contacted Doctor Fred Klenner and told him the terrible truth about his son.

By all accounts, Fritz went quite berserk when he was confronted with the news that his cover story had been blown. For him to lose that much face with his father, in the one area of passion and devotion they shared to an almost telepathic degree, was the worst thing in the world.

But Doctor Frederick Klenner, too, had a capacity to sustain fantasies. Once the explosion subsided, he did nothing to curb Fritz's career as a play-doctor. Fritz continued to wear his white smock and tote his little black bag, stethoscope dangling from the pocket.

For both men, the gap between what Fritz wanted to be, what Doc wanted him to be, and what Fritz really was, deep inside, was by now too great to be bridged except by a mutually sustained illusion. Living with his father's acceptance, if not exactly his blessing, was all that mattered to Fritz. Meanwhile, having his son around, still worshipful, still going through the motions of doctoring with the mimicking skill of an accomplished actor, was still important to the old man. The only version of reality that both men (and Mrs. Klenner, too, from what little she has said about these things) could now accept was a kind of crypto-reality that could not be validated by the outside world.

Fritz continued, therefore, to work at Doctor Fred's clinic in Reidsville. The patients were none the wiser, and most were every bit as happy to be treated by Young Doctor Klenner as by the real McCoy.

Of course, Fritz would sometimes vanish, without warning, for weeks at a time. Maybe he went back to Durham, where he still kept his apartment as a kind of "safe house." To his several girlfriends, all he would say was that he was involved in secret work for the Army. Or the Agency. Or the Royal Canadian Mounties. What did it matter? When he suddenly just up and vanished for a few days or weeks, it was surely for reasons he could not divulge due to oaths of secrecy and so forth.

How much of this rubbish Fred Klenner was aware of, and how much he chose to actually believe, is something that can never be known. Most parents want to see their children in the most flattering possible light, and if Fred Klenner managed to balance the contradictions in a way that enabled him to continue loving his only son, perhaps he can't be wholly condemned for it.

And if the patients at Doctor Fred's clinic wanted to call Fritz "Young Doctor Klenner," fully believing he would someday take over from his beloved father, well, Doctor Fred wanted to believe that, too.

The Late, Great Planet Earth

Armageddon has never been the big business it is today. The television evangelists hawk it, writers like Hal Lindsay have made fortunes writing about it, and there is even a considerable body of evidence that Ronald Reagan believes in it. And it's hard to refute. Nuclear weapons make it a possible future. No rational person can deny that.

But it's another thing entirely to literally believe in the imminent reality of the Apocalypse. That belief can tip you right over the edge of a cliff. If somebody says to you, "Nuclear war could mean the end of civilization as we know it," well, you nod your head and mutter, "Yes, I suppose it could." But if the same person goes on to tell you, "By the way, space aliens are putting hallucinogens in our drinking water," then watch out. You may be dealing with somebody who not only thinks The End is near, but who also *wants* it to happen. Someone, indeed, whose best hope for personal fulfillment lies in mass destruction.

There is a certain logic to the idea that, if civilization *is* going to collapse, you ought to start making preparations. It follows that if you are really prepared for it, you may not only survive, but even emerge on the other side as one of the ruling elite. For someone who feels utterly out of sync with things as they are now, that's a powerful fantasy.

Of course, as viewed by the rest of us, the problem is that everybody else's reality has got to go: political systems, economic systems, cultures, laws, moral conventions, restraints — all of it. The extreme survivalist world-view is totally beyond the boundaries of any functioning socioeconomic system.

Even on a personal level, Armageddon can be a very dangerous thing to flirt with. A person loses all ordinary restraints. The situation longed for is so extraordinary that existing standards just melt down and disappear. Fortunately no one person has the power to impose such fantasies on an entire society; usually, all an individual can do is bring about a private, personal, apocalypse. That's probably why people like Fritz Klenner seem to get so fascinated with Adolf Hitler, the one man who was in exactly the right place, time, and country to create an Armageddon-like effect far beyond the radius of his own family and community.

If you think of a family as a microcosm of society, then Fritz's arrival within my family was a close analog to the rise of hard-core terrorists in the world today. Abu Abbas is an avatar of Fritz Klenner's apocalyptic fantasies. Like Fritz, the new generation of pure terrorists performs acts which make no sense when viewed from the outside, acts that no longer seem to have any genuine political meaning because they are so totally self-referential.

And recall that there was something about the way Fritz talked about *his* version of Armageddon that disturbed even the neo-Nazis he ran around with while he pretended to be enrolled at Duke. When a bunch of self-proclaimed American Nazis tries to have you put away, then you are, I submit, in serious trouble.

CHAPTER FIFTEEN

Renewed Acquaintances

Susie Newsom Lynch's physical condition, more than her state of mind, gave cause for concern once she was back in the family's bosom after her return from Taiwan in mid-1980. She was listless, short tempered, and her color was bad. At Florence Newsom's urging, Susie went for a checkup at Doc Klenner's office in Reidsville.

Susie was examined by her cousin Fritz, who promptly (and inaccurately) rendered his diagnosis: multiple sclerosis. Doc Klenner seconded the diagnosis, even though he performed none of the usual exhaustive tests needed to zero in on the disease. MS does not announce itself with any unmistakable symptoms, but must usually be tracked down by a long process of elimination.

Susie was immediately started on a regimen of massive vitamin B injections. Most of the time, it was Fritz who administered the needle. Gradually, their childhood acquaintance renewed itself. She had never paid much attention to Fritz before, even though they were first cousins. He was, after all, six years younger than she, and he had always seemed a little strange.

But for some reason he didn't seem strange to her now. In fact, the more Susie talked with Fritz, the more sense he made. He was enrolled at Duke Medical School, he told her, and he was being groomed as Young Doctor Klenner to take over his father's practice.

Ol' Doc Fred was often within earshot, but he never said a word to correct his son's distortions.

Susie's health slowly improved as she put more time between herself and the abortive, depressing period in Taiwan. She gave credit for her improvement to the Klenners' doctoring. She enrolled again at Wake Forest University in Winston-Salem, this time working toward a degree in anthropology. She even began dating again.

But clouds were beginning to gather in another quarter. In the late spring of 1981, Tom Lynch borrowed some money from his mother and offered a property settlement to Susie via her divorce lawyer. The first round of negotiations collapsed, however, when the litigants could not decide who was responsible for a student loan Susie had taken out.

By the autumn of 1981, Tom Lynch had abandoned whatever faint hope of reconciliation there may have been. And it had been two years since he'd seen his sons. On September 16, his Albuquerque lawyer filed suit to settle the matter of visitation rights once and for all. Tom just wanted to get the whole mess behind him and start renewing his relationship with his two boys.

Susie didn't want him to see the boys at all — not now, and not ever, if she could help it. She then became terrified that he might obtain custody. But all Tom wanted was to *see* them.

The case became a legal football as the various aspects (visitation, property rights, the fine points of the divorce itself) were kicked back and forth between the courts in New Mexico and North Carolina.

Tom Lynch finally won permission to see the boys over Christmas, 1981, but only after he had posted a $10,000 bond to secure his promise to have them back in Susie's hands by the time agreed upon. It was a wretchedly brief visit, from the point of view of a man who had not seen his sons in two years, lasting only from December 22 to January 1.

Meanwhile, Susie's romance with a man she had been dating cooled by the autumn of 1981. And Susie herself seemed to be growing increasingly overwrought. She fussed and bothered over the boys more than ever. The bad times they had all shared in Taiwan had made her realize that she was blessed with two great kids, and there were signs that she was now trying to compensate for the guilt she felt about having roughed them up during the New Mexico days.

A parent who injures a child in anger often carries an internal wound that rarely stops bleeding. It is possible, however, to close such a wound. One way is by a hardening of the heart that leads to further insensitivity or cruelty. The other way is perpetual over-compensation, and that's the approach Susie seems to have taken. She monitored the boys' health with a zeal that bordered on fanaticism, and she took ostentatious care to let the neighbors see what a concerned mother she was.

At the same time, Susie lacked the focus necessary to finish any of her academic projects. Each time she returned to the educational system, including the Chinese interlude, her attention span grew shorter and the circumstances of her quitting became more defensive, more angry. Now she washed her hands of anthropology as well, cursing her teachers for fools. After a while, though, she tried again, this time enrolling in business education courses at the University of North Carolina at Greensboro.

Finally, in July 1982, Tom Lynch got his day in court and was permitted to take the boys back to New Mexico for a single three-week visit. Later that fall, Tom was awarded visitation rights of 35 days each summer. But because the boys were under age, the judge also ordered, at Susie's insistence, that an adult had to go with them on at least one leg of the two-stage airplane flight from Winston-Salem to Albuquerque. Tom thought he had been sandbagged by this expensive and unnecessary stipulation. The airlines, after all, had extremely reliable shepherding services for small children on connecting flights.

Tom Lynch did receive a Christmas present of a sort in 1982, however. His divorce from Susie came through.

The courtroom battles had been long, bitter, hard-fought, and expensive. Throughout them all, Susie had railed at Tom Lynch's mother, Delores, who was helping Tom handle the crippling legal costs (though not nearly as much as Susie thought she was). Susie expressed a deep and virulent hatred for Delores Lynch that other people could not comprehend. How could Susie speak so rabidly about a woman she had only seen a dozen or so times since her wedding day twelve years before?

Tom was even worse, Susie said to anybody who would listen. Tom was going to try to kidnap the boys. He could do it, too, because he was deeply involved with South American drug dealers as well as the Las Vegas mafia. The people who knew Tom Lynch thought he was a decent, hard-working dentist who was desperately trying to be a good father to the two children he still loved very deeply — but that was all an illusion, Susie explained. A friend who was a CIA agent had told her the truth.

At the final divorce settlement, in December 1982, Susie's first cousin, Fritz Klenner, was seen hanging around the courtroom. Nobody thought much about it at the time.

Kissin' Cousins

Fritz and Susie were not Bonnie and Clyde. To this day, I remain unconvinced that the sexual element in their relationship was all that important.

I used to believe there wasn't any sexual element, period. But then our private investigations turned up a couple of folks who had actually seen them necking when nobody else was home and they thought nobody was looking, so I guess it would be pretty naive to keep on believing that they never, ever, slept together.

But I still maintain that it could not have been a major part of the glue that bonded Fritz and Susie together. To have physical relations with one's first cousin was something that, in Susie's mind, would have carried unbelievably severe strictures and penalties. It *was* a passionate relationship, yes, in the sense that they were bound together by vivid delusions. But virtually everybody who saw them together has commented that you just could not detect any undercurrent of erotic attraction whatever. I don't think there was very much room for it.

You get mixed reviews about Fritz sexually. According to the few people who were in a position to know and who were willing to talk about it, he could, on occasion, be an inspired lover: imaginative and vigorous and attentive to mood. On the other hand, it appears that there were frequent, unpredictably long, periods of time during which he manifested absolutely no interest in sex. He would always explain this in terms of the pressures of his "work," his super-secret activities for whatever agency or outfit he was pretending to work for that month. And of course, since the women he slept with believed all that stuff about secret agencies, at least at first, it was not possible to press him about the matter. Everything was top secret. It was not exactly impotence so much as intense preoccupation or distraction. I think it would be accurate to describe him as not a highly sexed individual. For him, most erotic activity was ancillary, and strictly subordinate to, the psychological scenarios he was directing and starring in.

Fritz had always been drawn to troubled, vulnerable, recently divorced or separated women. He had a long and fairly sleazy track record in that regard. With Susie, although it probably started out the same way, it soon evolved into something wholly different. With her, he really wanted to be Saint George, the Protector.

It fed his ego to be able to take care of her, to have her seek shelter under the psychological umbrella he had popped open over her head. She represented the "proper" side of the family, the Sharps, and all the conventional middle-class virtues they stood for. This was Fritz's big chance to prove that he was better able to provide for their darling "Susie Q" than they were.

He probably drew immense satisfaction, too, from the idea that ol' Doc Fred was looking down from heaven and cheering him on. It was one of the few things Fritz could do, after his father died in 1984, that had already received his father's tacit blessing in life.

Both my mother and my father felt that Doc Klenner and his wife, Annie Hill, encouraged my sister's estrangement from the Newsom-Sharp side of the family. The undercurrents of tension between the two factions had been simmering more or less in the open for years. The snickering at Fred and his family and their curious ways had created a kind of cumulative pressure dome of resentment.

I don't mean for a moment to suggest that there was any kind of pre-planned strategy on the part of Frederick Klenner and Annie Hill to alienate Susie from her own parents. They would probably have expressed sincere indignation if anyone had suggested such a thing. It's just that circumstances placed Susie in their orbit when Fritz began treating her for her alleged case of multiple sclerosis. And they had all warmed to her, just as they had done when she was a little girl before most of the family feuding got started. They could tell that she returned their affection, and found it gratifying that Susie seemed to prefer their advice to that of her own parents, especially that of her own mother.

So, in the beginning, the drawing-together of Fritz and Susie could be explained in terms of circumstances and intra-family dynamics. But because Susie's incipient mental illness meshed so perfectly with Fritz's well-developed madness, what probably began as a sincere impulse on his part grew very sick, very quickly.

CHAPTER SEVENTEEN

Casting Off

Looking back on it later, Robert Newsom III viewed the start of Fritz Klenner's influence on his sister from the day Susie began circulating those wild tales about her husband, Tom Lynch, seemingly pulling the stories out of thin air. When Susie ranted about Tom that way, and people asked her, incredulously, where she had obtained her information, Susie merely spoke darkly of a "family friend" who was an undercover agent — sometimes for the FBI, sometimes for the CIA. Fritz had figured her out and was already putting his moves on her. She was wide open for it.

The Newsom family began to wonder what was happening to their beloved Susie Q. Once so bright, so vivacious, so engaged by life's possibilities, she now seemed eaten up with bile, malice, and frustration.

There was no sudden dramatic moment when the family realized that Fritz was becoming Susie's closest companion. His presence just gradually impinged on everyone's awareness late in 1982. Little by little, the Newsoms started to feel decidedly uncomfortable about Fritz. Ol' Doc Klenner may have been a bit weird, but he was the one great eccentric without whom no large Southern family can function. And for all of his dubious medical theories, and the reactionary slant of his political beliefs, he was still a healer. But Fritz more and more came to seem like an embodiment and exaggeration of all his father's weirdness — without the elder Klenner's compensating goodness, warmth, and dedication.

At the time Fritz began growing close to Susie, he was dating three other women. Two of the three were troubled women emerging from failed marriages. Two of the three had adolescent or pre-adolescent children. He had different stories for each of them, at different times, about his work, his past, and his physical condition.

During this period, Susie and her two sons were living with her mother and father, Florence and Bob Newsom Jr. As Florence began to observe the growing relationship between Susie and Fritz, she reacted with a mother's instincts. To begin with, she thought there was something decidedly peculiar about a man who would habitually stalk the streets of a somnolent little town like Reidsville wearing camouflage clothes and a K-Bar survival knife. And if she found it impossible to relate to Fritz's macho posturing, she found it quite incomprehensible that Susie, whose taste in men and culture had always been so fastidious, could be attracted to such a Neanderthal lifestyle. Florence was also disturbed that her grandsons, John and Jim, were showing signs of becoming infatuated with Uncle Fritz's military fetish.

At first, Florence Newsom simply could not bring herself to believe there was any romantic attraction between her nephew Fritz and her daughter Susie. But when Fritz started dropping by the house at odd hours, acting more like a suitor than a friendly relation, it got Florence's attention. And when Florence found out that Fritz had started spending the night, on weekends when she and Bob were visiting Hattie in Old Town, she was scandalized.

Florence contacted her sister, Annie Hill, who was Fritz's mother. Florence wanted a mom-to-mom discussion to enlist her aid in defusing the difficult situation. But Annie Hill, with the vagueness that seems to have characterized all of her dealings with problems created by Fritz's activities, allowed as how she didn't see any problem at all. She did not, in fact, seem terribly interested in even discussing the matter. So Florence had it out directly with Susie, and later had a one-on-one confrontation with Fritz that must have scorched the paint off the walls.

Whatever was going on with Fritz, Florence told her daughter, it was not going to continue under the family roof. Fine, Susie fired back. Whereupon she packed up, collected the children, and left. Susie rented an apartment in the Friendly Hills development on the west side of Greensboro, near Guilford College. For a period of some weeks, Bob and Florence had no idea of their daughter's whereabouts.

Susie was in a snit, no doubt about it. She spurned all efforts at reconciliation with her mother. She treated Florence, now, with the same sort of coldly furious disdain she used to reserve for her mother-in-law, Delores Lynch. Checks sent to Susie's address were torn up. Gifts sent to the two children were refused or returned unopened. Susie also distanced herself from the other members of the family, including her grandmother Hattie and Aunt Su-Su — the supreme court justice whom she admired, probably, more than anyone else on earth.

Susie's protectiveness toward the boys became obsessive. She stayed with them at the school bus stop each morning until they were picked up, so nobody could snatch them from the curb. She sketched maps of their school, showing which classrooms they occupied at any hour of the day, so she could sweep them out of harm's way without losing a minute. She bought first one, then two, big chow dogs, as a kind of first line of defense against intruders who might show up at the apartment.

While Susie was casting off from her side of the family and gravitating into the Klenners' orbit, Tom Lynch married his former dental assistant, Kathy Anderson, in June 1983. Not long after that, his two sons arrived in New Mexico for their now annual summertime visit.

Tom was saddened and disgusted by their appearance. Their teeth were coated with grunge and their arms looked like those of hardcore drug-shooters, so black and blue were they from all the hypos full of vitamins Fritz had been injecting into them. They were silent and morose. They never spoke about friends their own age, and it gradually dawned on Tom that they didn't have any. Susie wouldn't let them out of the apartment unless it was absolutely necessary.

John had inherited his father's predilection for sports, but he was never allowed to do anything outside of school activities other than go on camping trips with Uncle Fritz. Jim, the more poetic and dreamy of the two, was a good-natured boy with a natural gift for making friends. He was the kind of child a teacher remembers long after his classmates have faded into anonymity.

Tom's mother, Delores Lynch, was as frustrated as her son. She had been making homemade goodies for her grandsons and sending them to Susie's Greensboro apartment all spring. But Susie had commandeered the packages and thrown them out without letting the boys sample the contents. They might contain poison, she said.

Finally, toward the end of the boys' summer visit in New Mexico, Tom arranged for them to spend some time with Delores. She loosened up greatly and seemed to really enjoy their company. Delores concluded that Tom deserved more visitation time — and that she did, too.

It was an idea that would cost Delores Lynch her life.

Incident in a Parking Lot

It was in early 1983 that Susie moved into her own apartment in Greensboro. Mother told me there had been a number of conversations between herself and Annie Hill, conversations that grew increasingly confrontational. Mother asked Annie Hill about Susie's supposed case of multiple sclerosis, about whether or not Fritz was really any kind of doctor. She never got a concrete answer to any of those questions. Annie Hill would never confirm anything about the exact status of Fritz's medical training, and she refused to discuss Susie's condition unless Susie gave her permission — which, by this time, Susie refused to do. Annie did admit that the original MS diagnosis had been made by Fritz (that comforted Mother a whole lot!), but that Doctor Klenner would back him up all the way. The net result of these conversations was to confirm my mother's suspicions that some kind of funny business was going on.

It was not until 1984, I think, that my parents realized the true extent of the rift between them and Susie, the true scope of the problem they had. But when they realized that this was not just another one of Susie's giant pouts, a sense of alarm began to creep into their minds.

In May 1984, when Doctor Klenner died, the rest of the family finally learned, without equivocation, that Fritz had no medical degree and no prospect of ever getting one. It was, I think, in the late summer of 1984 that Justice Susie Sharp called Terry Sanford (then president of Duke University and now a U.S. senator) and asked him to check on whether or not Fritz had ever, at any time, been enrolled at Duke Medical School. The answer was no. She also made inquiries to the North Carolina Board of Medical Examiners, with the same results. They'd never heard of Fritz Klenner.

The depth of the rift between my mother and sister was illustrated by something that happened when my wife took Mother grocery shopping one day. Inside the supermarket, Florence spotted her grandchildren, John and Jim Lynch, in a nearby aisle. It had been a long time since she'd seen the kids, so she broke out into a huge grin and went over to them.

Then Susie swooped down like a protective eagle, grabbed the boys by the napes of their necks, and bundled them roughly into her car. My wife had known Florence for years, but that moment, as Susie drove angrily away, leaving mother standing there in the parking lot, was the first time she had ever seen my mother cry.

CHAPTER NINETEEN

Death Comes to the Good Doctor

During the autumn and winter of 1983-84, Fritz Klenner withdrew from his other personal relationships and concentrated on Susie. He escaped one inconvenient affair by claiming that his work had become more demanding. He would be going undercover for a long time, doing dirty and dangerous stuff. It was too risky, and too sensitive, for him to involve anyone else.

His father, Doctor Frederick Klenner, died on May 20, 1984, at the age of 76. Later, to some people, Fritz would brag about the heroic medical measures he had taken to save his father's life, couching the stories in terms of a fierce struggle with the Grim Reaper himself. But in truth, Doctor Klenner's ticker just stopped, and there wasn't a thing Fritz could do about it.

His father's death tore into Fritz's elaborate weave of fantasy, robbing him forever of any chance to revel in his father's pride. Fritz learned, from the pain he experienced at his father's passing, the power of death to transform the shape and texture of all that surrounds a person.

From there, it was only a quick leap to the conclusion that even the most extreme fantasies can be nudged toward actualization by the selective application of death. An environment can be given new patterns, new priorities. Obstacles and problems can be erased as if they had never existed.

When Fritz's former survivalist buddies (the ones who had informed on him to the SBI) heard that Doctor Klenner was dead, they felt that the old man's demise would trigger some serious craziness in Fritz. Doctor Klenner had been an anchor to reality, a center of gravity, at times a kind of external conscience. When Doctor Klenner died, Fritz's fuse started to burn. The only question was the length of that fuse.

Fritz's determination to succeed in his role of play-doctor was enormous. Whatever his Daddy wanted him to be, that was what Fritz would try to become. But the sad, sorry, fact of the matter was that Fritz just didn't have the right stuff, intellectually, to make it in medical school.

You could see it in his handwriting: loose, wide-open loops in the curves of his letters, a halting and uncertain syntax in his sentences, gross misspellings of common words. To be sure, these weaknesses are not themselves signs of a disordered mind. Many people in the medical profession do not exactly write in Jeffersonian copperplate. But the sheer laziness and weak basic skills did indicate a lack of discipline.

As long as Doctor Klenner was alive, he acquiesced to Fritz's play-doctor fantasies. Unethical, perhaps, but not criminal. All he allowed Fritz to do was talk to the patients and give injections, functions that most people could learn to handle with a certain degree of finesse. There is certainly nothing to indicate that Doctor Klenner ever allowed Fritz to actually perform surgery on anyone.

As long as Doc was around — giving the boy some freedom to play at being a doctor, but still keeping an eye on him so it wouldn't get out of hand — Fritz's lid stayed screwed on. Fritz's activities couldn't become too antisocial without incurring his father's displeasure, so he seems to have limited his sociopathic behavior to his personal relationships outside of the confines of Reidsville. As long as Daddy was alive, Fritz played the games Daddy permitted him to play, and largely played them according to the ground rules Daddy maintained. If Fritz was not exactly a productive member of society, he was at least working to maintain outward respectability.

For a while, after his father's death, Fritz continued to treat patients at Doc's clinic. Justice Susie Sharp, however, finally blew the whistle on her nephew's charade. She called former North Carolina Governor Terry Sanford, who was then president of Duke University, and asked him to investigate Fritz's records there. Fritz, of course, had no records at Duke or anywhere else within the legitimate medical establishment.

Justice Sharp then contacted Fritz's mother and explained to her in forceful terms just what the penalties were for practicing medicine without a license. More official communications were sent to the Klenners' family attorney. Soon the doors of the clinic were closed for good.

And patients began wondering what had happened to the kind and comforting Young Doctor Klenner.

The Only Thing in the World That Mattered

The question that comes immediately to mind, of course, is how did Fritz Klenner get away with such an elaborate con-job for so long? Maybe the best place to start dealing with that is with the clinical definition of a sociopathic personality.

All of the textbooks give similar characteristics. Such individuals tend to act out their inner conflicts on the stage of their family environment; they flaunt the normal rules of social behavior; and they are often wildly impulsive (Fritz sometimes spent two or three thousand dollars in cash at military surplus stores, or would go into an all-night supermarket and buy a ten-year supply of cocoa at two o'clock in the morning).

Sociopaths are utterly amoral, and most of the time they are unable to forego quick gratification of their desires. They tolerate frustration poorly. They are incapable of deep and lasting affection, yet their ability to charm, and to seem plausible to others, is often highly developed and remarkably subtle. They are quite successful at manipulating people to their own ends.

Opposing this type of personality is likely to elicit aggression, hostility, even serious violence. Their antisocial behavior is never compromised by guilt or remorse, because they have such a strong capacity for rationalizing and blaming their own behavior on other people.

Repeated failures and punishments rarely improve either their behavior or their judgment. The worst symptoms seem to appear in individuals who share inherited factors from an antisocial male and a hysterical female relative. There may be a history of emotional strife between the parents, and between the parents and the wider circle of relations. Such individuals are often deeply paranoiac, and they deal with it by projecting their own hostilities and conflicts onto those with whom they regularly come into contact.

It is absolutely wrong to look at Fritz Klenner as some kind of simple-minded thug. When you listen to him talking on police surveillance tapes, you realize that you're listening to one of the coolest customers who ever lived. Just think of it: Here was a man who had managed to con his own parents for years into believing that he was in medical school.

His parents were predisposed to believe him, of course, but I know for a fact that Fritz managed to pull the same con, over long periods of time, with other doctors, pharmacists, and with all manner of intelligent, well-educated people. I know of one judge who, when introduced to Fritz, found him thoroughly credible. And this was a judge who had spent many years in criminal court, who had encountered every kind of slick, shady character and con artist you can imagine. This judge was a strong, subtle, and finely discerning evaluator of human character, and a man, moreover, whose years on the bench had given him a fairly cynical and jaundiced view of human nature in general.

Virtually everybody who came in contact with Fritz (at least during the period when he was still reasonably in control of himself) had no trouble believing that he was indeed what he purported to be.

Fritz Klenner was a virtuoso imposter, whether he was dealing with pillars of society, lonely housewives, or redneck gun-nuts. Ironically, about the only category of people he didn't try to con was the very group he most wanted to be accepted by, outside of the medical profession — real combat veterans. Only a small percentage of the survivalist extremists are actual combat veterans. Few Vietnam vets are interested in ever playing soldier again, and they could easily detect Fritz's lies. He always shied away from real veterans, or at least kept his mouth shut about his "battle experiences" while they were within earshot.

Character traits which were muted, repressed, or very sporadic in his parents — antisocial behavior and a tendency to hysteria, punctuated on rare occasions by violent outbursts — were reproduced and magnified many-fold in Fritz. When his whole elaborate construct fell apart, when he was unmasked by evidence that he could neither refute nor escape, he did not respond with remorse, or pleas for understanding and forgiveness. What happened instead was a psychic explosion. According to the stories that circulated in the family after people started coming forward to tell what they knew, his response when confronted with irrefutable evidence of his lies and deceptions was uncontrolled raging, screaming, and operatic pistol-waving.

God knows what kind of madhouse scene it must have been up there in the clinic when things came boiling to a head. According to the tales that circulated through the family, Fritz really went berserk — throwing things down the stairs and even threatening his parents with physical harm.

After one of these explosions would subside within the walls of the clinic, however, Doc and Annie Hill Klenner drew their wagons into a circle and tried to shield both Fritz and the family's reputation from the outside world. Whatever it did to them to learn that their son was a liar and a con-man, it would have been a thousand times worse to have that knowledge broadcast to outsiders. They permitted the illusion that he was a medical student to continue for years, and encouraged their patients to think that Young Doctor Klenner was indeed being groomed to take over the clinic when Doc retired. And Fritz lied about those things all the time in his father's presence without once being contradicted. One shudders to think of the psychological toll that must have been exacted.

Think what emotions must have been building up inside Fritz over the years, just from trying to maintain such an elaborate and many-sided hoax. Every day when he woke up, he must have looked in the mirror and asked himself: Is this the day I will be unmasked?

Fritz Klenner was not the only son of a doctor who could not be a doctor himself. What's unusual is that he never entertained the possibility of being anything else. It was as if he must be a doctor, just like Daddy, or nothing at all.

It would all have been different, perhaps, if Fritz had somehow managed to get a medical degree from *somewhere* — that place in Grenada, or the Poppa Doc College of Medicine in Haiti, or something. What he needed to stay balanced was some positive feedback from the outside world, something solidly based on external reality. He never got any.

If he had somehow managed to earn a real medical degree, his self-esteem and sense of self-worth would have received an enormous boost. But even that might not have solved his problems in the long run.

It is dangerous to base all of your self-esteem on things external to your identity as a human being. After all, there *are* unsuccessful doctors. Just getting a license to practice medicine is only the first step of a career, not the culmination of one.

Suppose you were Fritz and you *had* become a doctor, and you defined yourself in terms of the size of your practice, the BMW in the carport, the tax shelters in the portfolio, the house in the best neighborhood. Then suppose, years later, you came up against the fact that you were not going to be terribly successful. Or suppose, years later, you start making mistakes. Then would come this terrible realization that all those outward perks could slip away from you. And suppose, on top of that, you had long-simmering psychological problems to begin with. That, surely, is a recipe for problems.

For Fritz, all sense of self-worth, even the nature of reality itself, emanated from his father. Then, *whammo!*, one day Daddy is gone, and not only do you have to deal with that trauma, but you also have to admit that you never, ever, became anything like what he had wanted you to be.

It's when Fritz came up against that brick wall — the immutable fact that not only could he never *be* a doctor, but he could no longer even *pretend* to be a doctor — it is at that point, I'll bet my last dime on it, that he embraced the apocalyptic creed in its most literal form. He crossed the line from fantasizing about it to actually believing it was a fact.

Look at it this way: If he couldn't be a doctor on *this* side of the holocaust, maybe he could be one of the saviors of the whole white race on the *other* side of it.

More than that: If the apocalypse did come, Fritz would indeed have found himself in demand as a doctor. Fritz had soaked up a lot of practical medical knowledge by simply hanging around the clinic all those years. He would have been at least as handy to have in a guerilla outfit as your average pharmacist's mate, probably a lot more handy. Someone with his degree of skill could treat maybe ninety percent of the injuries and illnesses that normally plague mankind. Of course, he couldn't perform open-heart surgery, but he could sew up a wound, bind a splint, administer shots, extract a bullet, deliver a baby, and tell you what pills to take when you got sick.

On the other side of the big event, Fritz would suddenly be able to see himself not as an abject failure, but as a very valuable member of post-holocaust society. Here is a medic who also has a working knowledge of firearms, camouflage, explosives, map-reading, foraging, Ninja stalking techniques, and who could also field-strip an M-16 in the dark.

Maybe he wasn't as good as Doc Klenner in the operating theater, but he was a hell of a lot better out on the firing range (and I've been shooting with both men). If the big bang really did wipe out civilization, Fritz Klenner would have had his golden chance to put it all together again. He would have been even better than his father: more useful, more versatile, more effective.

But only *if* the end really came — and he must have known it. But then, hadn't Doc told him that things were coming to an end? "Fritz, my boy, life as we know it is going to be shattered into a thousand fragments…all the signs are there, all the stars are in the right places." Doc Klenner intimated, on many occasions, that he had precise knowledge of when the fire would rain down and the Negroes would stage their insurrection. "You can know," he would say. "If you know how to read the signs, you can know." But he was kind of cagey about it. Naturally, Fritz would push him for more precise information, but Doc would just shake his head sadly and say that maybe it was better not to know in advance.

I think Fritz felt okay about himself when he started looking at the universe from that angle. After all, so much is required to get ready for the collapse of civilization. There isn't going to be time for honest-to-God medical school, and, hey, what difference would it make anyway if he graduated? Three or four years down the road, when all the hospitals and medical schools are just piles of radioactive rubble, a medical degree wouldn't be worth the paper it was printed on.

But the medical *knowledge* would be. In fact, if you grant that Fritz had really convinced himself that things-as-we-know-them were falling to pieces, and that if the Apocalypse were going to happen pretty soon, then a whole lot of what Fritz did suddenly appears consistent and logical and rational. All that gear he acquired, all that self-training he put himself through, all those how-to-survive manuals he read. If you grant him just that one big assumption, then the man appears to have been proceeding in a reasonable and orderly way.

If Armageddon really was around the corner, at a time when most young medical school graduates were just finishing their residency requirement, Fritz was actually way ahead of all of them and was in a far better program of study. Given the Armageddon premise, his actions reveal internal consistency.

This was a weak fall-back position, of course, but it was the only place he could go once his father had died.

The demons were loose in Fritz now, and Doc wasn't around any more to sling holy water into the darkness.

Mind Games

In late 1984, Tom Lynch notified Susie's lawyer (as he was required to do under the terms of the visitation agreement) that he would be coming to visit the boys in Greensboro for about a week in November. I think from Tom's point of view, the visit was a success. He got to spend a little "quality time" with his sons, and he was able to talk with my mother and father, and also with several of the Sharps, and consolidate their support for his campaign to win more visitation rights.

I had no idea how far beyond reason my sister had gone until one day when she showed up unannounced at my office, not too long before Tom Lynch's arrival. She looked so wild and disheveled that I could hear the note of alarm in my receptionist's voice when she announced Susie's visit.

Tom's imminent trip to Greensboro had really spooked her out, she said, and there were some things she had to get off her chest. Then she began itemizing things that struck me not as simply disturbed, but actually deluded. Until now, Susie's behavior had been mystifying, saddening, sometimes irritating. But now, for the first time, I understood just how out of touch with reality she could become.

Item: Delores and Janie Lynch, who had been viciously murdered at their home in Kentucky that July, had been killed by the Colombian cocaine mafia, acting through the Las Vegas branch of the American mafia. According to Susie, Tom Lynch had close connections with the killers. How did she know? She knew it because Fritz had told her so, and Fritz knew it because he worked for the CIA and had inside sources for that kind of information.

Item: She had tried to tell the authorities about the truth behind the Lynch murders, but they wouldn't listen to her. Who had she tried to tell? I asked. Oh, the Feds, and the Kentucky State Police, and maybe, she said, the North Carolina SBI, too. (In fact, as far as our private investigation has been able to determine, she had talked to nobody at any of these agencies. I doubt that she'd said any of these things to anyone else before she dumped it all in my lap that morning.)

Item: She feared for her life and for the lives of her two sons, because their names were surely on the same hit-list. At this point, to illustrate what she was saying, she reached into her handbag and brought out a little .25-caliber automatic, courtesy of guess who, and indicated that she'd been practicing a lot with it recently.

After hearing all this, I asked her a few questions about her relationship with Fritz. She insisted that the only thing going on between them was protective in nature. Fritz was just looking after her while all this sinister undercover stuff was happening on the edges of the family.

She was close to hysteria by the time she finished. I came away from the conversation convinced that my sister was seriously, not just harmlessly, deluded. Of course I informed my mother about the encounter, in detail. But I was worried about how my parents would take the information. I myself had suffered until recently from a serious brain condition associated with alcoholism and — even though I had made considerable progress and the prognosis was good — I was afraid they would take my information with a grain of salt. Actually, they believed me, but they just didn't know what to do with the information.

Looking back on the incident, which was like a curtain-raiser for the holocaust that was about to descend upon us, it occurs to me that Fritz probably manipulated Susie into making that visit. Perhaps the reasoning went like this: If he could, through Susie, convince me of the veracity of what he was saying about Tom Lynch and his underworld connections, then I would become their ally and would in turn

convince my mother and father. My parents, then, would stop helping Tom in his legal campaign to win more visitation rights.

I think Fritz and Susie had learned by this time that Tom had been
in close communication with my parents. This dramatic visit by
Susie was a means of indirectly exerting pressure on them. Fritz
probably said something to her like this: "Hey, look, Tom Lynch is
duping your parents into collusion with him about stealing the boys.
You know what would happen to the boys if the mob got hold of
them. Your parents won't listen to you, and they won't listen to me.
We gotta break through to them somehow, so let's try it through your
brother."

This was also the first time she had revealed, by name, the source
of all these dire accusations she'd been making about Tom Lynch.
Bells went off in my head at the sound of Fritz's name, and I guess I
should have paid more attention to them. But it was hard to take
Fritz seriously. I, too, am a gun enthusiast (though strictly interested
in hunting, not in man-killer hardware), and I've spent enough time
in places where a lot of firearms dealing goes on to have encountered
plenty of specimens of the particular kind of kook who gets drawn to
the company of gun-nuts. Some are 'Nam-droppers whose brains
got stuck in a groove back in the late Sixties, but most are young
dudes who were too young to fight there and who think everything
would have turned out differently if only *they* had been in the fight.
You run into these guys all the time, and they're usually the most
pathetic, ineffectual, harmless kooks you can imagine. I had Fritz
pegged the same way: one of those guys whose head is filled with
fantasies about pulling triggers and splashing brains on the wall, but
who would never actually *do* anything like that. I figured he was like
those men who fantasize about rape, but who would never go out
and really attack a woman.

Evidently, my response to Susie's visit encouraged her to make
another try some weeks later. I was at home by myself when Susie
appeared at the door, unannounced.

She had a photograph she'd torn out of either *Time* or *Newsweek*.
It was purportedly taken inside Nicaragua, and it showed a man with
a briefcase handing over some cash to a Contra delegation and

supervising the unloading of a supply plane, which you could see in the background.

The person in the photograph had his back to the camera, but Susie stabbed her finger at it, waved it under my nose, and insisted it was a picture of Fritz Klenner. I had to admit that from that angle, yeah, it did sort of look like Fritz's back. And his head was shaped like Fritz's head, and he had a beard, which Fritz had at that time. It was a close enough resemblance so that if I had seen the same back at a crowded party, I might have been tempted to yell "Hey, Fritz!" So I didn't argue with her, I just mumbled something like, "Well, er, yeah, I guess it does sorta look as though it could be Fritz."

It was just another one of his little mind games. I can just see him running over to her with this copy of *Time* and saying: "Uh-oh, now my cover's blown!" And, of course, Fritz did absent himself without explanation for long periods of time whenever he got the urge to go off and be mysterious. It would not have taken much effort to convince Susie that he was making courier runs into Contraland. Since anyone who read the papers knew that the CIA was employing some very odd and questionable types to do its dirty work down there — like Eugene Hasenfus — the idea that Fritz was involved wasn't wildly implausible. I'm sure Susie bought it right away.

What Fritz was really doing, by showing her that picture and setting up that scenario in her head, was motivating her to show it to me, so that it would lend legitimacy to all the stuff she'd been telling me about Tom Lynch's underworld connections. Here's proof. See, I *told* you Fritz was CIA, and there he is! And, honestly, I couldn't look Susie in the eye and say you're nuts, this could be anybody. It was a shrewd little number on Fritz's part, setting us up like that.

After all the killings, we did investigate the possibility that Fritz might really have maintained some connections with the spook world, perhaps doing courier work, or something low-level that required more zeal than discretion. But there is nothing. It was all fantasy.

The only reason we even gave him the benefit of a doubt is that he *did* make some astounding statements from time to time. Most of them could not be verified, of course, without top-level security clearance — stories about a Russian submarine sinking off North Carolina's Outer Banks, that kind of thing. But then a couple of days before the Russians actually landed their paratroops at the Kabul airport, he bragged about having inside knowledge about a Russian invasion of Afghanistan.

And then there was the Grenada invasion on October 25, 1983. I still don't know what to make of that. He predicted the invasion would happen, and he predicted the date, and he even predicted the general operational plan. Now, there weren't many people who were privy to that kind of information at that point, and Fritz was right on the money about it. That kind of thing happened often enough to impress a good number of people, to make them think he really was some kind of secret agent. At some point in the gray zone between his fantasy life and the cold, hard world of real-life intelligence work, there was a sporadic interface that enabled him to pick up this kind of scuttlebutt, seemingly out of the air.

The most plausible theory is that some of the right-wing fringe groups he hung around with in the Fort Bragg area may have had sources inside the Army base, and that Fritz picked up these little tidbits from his friends in the various paramilitary groups that keep sprouting like barnacles around Fayetteville. Alternatively, he might have been having an affair with some high-ranking officer's wife, although I doubt very much if anyone is going to rush forward now and confirm that theory.

In the last few months of Fritz and Susie's relationship, after they started living together full-time, the mind games between them were just incredible.

Shortly after she and Tom Lynch had a bitter telephone argument about visitation rights — a phone call whose contents, you may be sure, were instantly and vividly communicated to Fritz — Susie returned to the apartment, alone, and discovered two of the boys' favorite stuffed animals with their throats cut open. These were the boys' "travel animals," special-occasion toys reserved for their trips to visit their father in New Mexico. Fritz knew this, of course, and could not have picked a more savagely disturbing way to inflame Susie's paranoia, and to increase her dependence on him.

Perhaps, though, the phone call she received not long after she discovered the mutilated animals — a few months after Delores and Jane Lynch were murdered — would qualify as more frightening than the mutilated toys. The phone rang, she answered, and a voice she could not identify whispered: "Two down and two to go . . . ."

"Two down" could only mean Delores and Jane Lynch. "Two to go" could only mean her children.

If it was indeed Fritz making the call, you might wonder, why didn't she recognize his voice? There are chapters in some of those books Fritz avidly collected which explain all about voice-disguise, basic training stuff for agents in the field. There are dozens of ways to effectively alter the timbre of your speech.

The pattern of Fritz's little head-benders was to first send a jolt of sheer terror coursing through Susie. After a while, when he figured she'd stewed long enough for him to reap the maximum benefit, he would suddenly appear, armed to the teeth, and she could relax and start to feel secure again.

A normal couple probably would have been driven apart very quickly by this kind of madness. But it just seemed to wind Fritz and Susie tighter and tighter.

CHAPTER TWENTY-TWO

Downward Spirals

When Doctor Frederick Klenner died in May 1984, he left Fritz a bequest of $25,000 cash from an insurance policy. On Tuesday, July 17, only five days before the Lynch murders, Fritz made his first big withdrawal from this inheritance. Another large chunk of the money helped Susie purchase a 1984 Blazer S-10, a smaller version of Fritz's own hulking, four-wheel-drive vehicle, a model that had received great reviews in the survivalist press. Fritz had converted his own Blazer into a survivalmobile, outfitting it with tools, a police scanner, a bank of halogen floodlights, a winch, a roll bar, first-aid gear, rations, ammunition, and, at some point, a powerful bomb — bolted to the floor beneath the front passenger seat. Just in case. So they couldn't take him alive.

Most of the rest of the money went for guns: assault rifles, shotguns, pistols, and a 9mm Israeli Uzi — a compact weapon which can be sold legally only in a semiautomatic configuration, unless the purchaser has the necessary (and expensive) federal licenses required to own automatic firearms. Fritz did not have such a license, and he had no intention of subjecting himself to even the cursory scrutiny that goes along with the application for one. Still, no problem: Fritz just went to his collection of mercenary magazines, looked up the address of one of the backroom companies that supplies conversion kits, ordered a few parts, slipped them into the mechanism, and voila! — the weapon was converted into a full-automatic submachine gun.

He also bought knives, packs, sleeping bags, uniforms, boots, flares, blasting caps, and hundreds of books, manuals, and pamphlets, covering everything from how to field-strip Communist bloc infantry weapons to the manufacture of homemade explosives and silencers. Over time, Fritz accumulated an impressive arsenal that eventually included 9 rifles, 11 shotguns, 16 pistols, 2 full-automatic weapons, 2 Claymore mines, 35 smoke and tear-gas grenades, canisters of Mace, numerous knives, cases of dynamite, black powder, an assortment of martial arts spikes and throwing stars, and more than 10,700 rounds of ammunition of various calibers and gauges. In fact, Fritz was better equipped than some small-town police departments.

While shopping for all of this gear — most of it readily available — he frequently hung out at the big military surplus stores in Greensboro, Winston-Salem, and Raleigh. Each time he went into the stores, he would buy hundreds of dollars' worth of merchandise, always paying cash, just as his father had done. The store managers soon learned to put up with his incessant and often contradictory boasts of martial prowess. One time, he was a contract operative for the CIA. The next time, he was a member of the top-secret Delta Force, the elite anti-terrorist unit from Fort Bragg. He was a veteran of clandestine ops both vital and dangerous. He ran a commando school in the woods near Doc Klenner's farm. He went on and on and on, for as long as anyone would listen. Most rational people just figured he was full of it.

But Susie thought Fritz was the only person she could trust anymore. Over and over again, like a litany, Susie poured out to Fritz her biggest fear: that Tom Lynch, aided by the money he'd inherited from his murdered mother and (the most immediate threat of all) the traitorous testimony of Bob and Florence Newsom, would succeed in wresting their two sons away from her.

Don't worry, Fritz told her; that's not going to happen. Fritz will take care of the problem.

Until March 1985, Fritz still rented, and spent time in, his Durham apartment, although the irregularity of his comings and goings make it hard to tell how much time he actually spent there. After he moved out of the Durham place, he moved in with Susie in

Greensboro. By that time, the nest was ready. Over time their relationship had been growing more intense, and Fritz had transformed Susie's Friendly Hills apartment into a hermetically sealed little world, as messy and piled with stuff as ol' Doc Klenner's house used to be.

Fritz recreated that childhood environment — except he stocked it with his own personal totems and fetishes. He hung crosses and draped camouflage sheets over the windows, posted mystic-religious incantations on the doors. He also booby-trapped the main entrance with a tear-gas canister. All that was missing was garlic hanging from the eaves, a silver crucifix, and a doctor's bag full of sharp wooden stakes.

Eventually, the apartment became so crammed with ammo cases and heaps of survivalist gear that there was scarcely any room left to walk and nowhere at all for more than two adults to sit down.

That was okay. They rarely welcomed visitors anymore.

Above, Fritz Klenner, 30, as "Young Doctor Klenner" in 1982. Left, Fritz's parents, Doctor Frederick C. Klenner and Annie Hill (Sharp) Klenner, in their clinic in 1982.

Fritz's yearbook picture at the end of junior year at Reidsville Senior High School. Fritz as a high school sophomore (above) and as a member of the library club (without glasses).

Susie Newsom.

Susie Newsom at her wedding to Tom Lynch in 1970.

Top, Robert III and
Susie with Robert Jr.
and Florence in the
1960s. Above, Robert
III in college. Left,
Florence Newsom.

Susie's boys, John and Jim
Lynch with their great aunt,
Justice Susie Sharp (top).
Susie's grandmother,
"Nana" Newsom. Robert
Newsom, Susie's father,
with his beloved roses.

Susie, John, and Jim in Taiwan.

Susie, John, and Jim.

The aftermath of tragedy. Ian Perkins on his way to court following the Newsom murders. Below, Tom Lynch, Susie's husband, an Albuquerque dentist.

A Jump She Could Not Make

There's an interesting difference between my outlook on the murders of Delores and Jane Lynch and the Kentucky State Police theory — a theory now shared, incidentally, by Tom Lynch. They reverse the priorities of responsibility, viewing Fritz as some kind of servant who did whatever my sister Susie told him to do, including going out and snuffing people. And they hold to this theory in spite of the tremendous body of evidence against it.

I don't think they've really closed the books on this case yet, over there in Kentucky. Detective Dan Davidson, I'll bet you, still wrestles with it from time to time. He's sort of my opposite number. Any new piece of evidence that turns up, he fits it into his conceptual framework. I do the same, of course.

Sandy Sands, Susie's attorney up in Reidsville who is now a state senator, remains convinced that Susie really did see the Kentucky slayings as a gangland hit that stemmed from Tom Lynch's supposed mobster/drug trafficker/KGB connections. Fritz had really implanted that idea in her mind and had her convinced that it was based on real information about real threats. That explains why she refused to permit the boys to stay with Tom for another week. She was genuinely terrified that John and Jim would be next on the hit list. That their father needed them very much after his mother and sister were killed wouldn't have mattered one bit compared to the paranoid convictions she was nurturing.

Sands remembers Susie as being truly "frantic" at the news of the Lynch killings, but only because of the possible repercussions where her sons were concerned. She didn't have a word of compassion for Delores and Janie Lynch.

Susie had reached a state where she could make these surgically exact emotional distinctions. She could be sincerely distraught and terrified for her kids, and at the same moment, relieved by the death of a woman whom she loathed and whose influence she feared.

For Fritz, the killing of the Lynches was a perfectly judged move. It was a kind of offering to Susie. By removing someone who had crossed her and who now threatened to thwart her will and frustrate her desires — and, at the same time, by escalating Susie's condition of delusion and paranoia — he had succeeded in binding her that much closer to him and to the protection he seemed to offer.

Fritz might have said, "It's just like I told you: The Colombian mafia's long arm reached out and struck down the Lynches." That the killings had happened at all might have been the final proof, if Susie still needed proof by this time, that Fritz knew what he was talking about and the dangers he had outlined were real.

Much later, the Kentucky State Police checked Susie's long-distance telephone records and discovered that she broke her constant pattern of calls to Fritz on the weekend the Lynches were murdered — she made no calls to his house on those days. From this the police concluded she was with Fritz when he made his deadly run to Kentucky.

That is a possibility, but I think it's a remote one. My sister's phone records would have revealed the same anomaly if she merely knew that Fritz had gone somewhere that weekend and could not be reached by phone. We know that Fritz was always disappearing for various lengths of time for various reasons. So the phone records alone don't prove anything one way or the other, and a good trial lawyer could knock down that part of the Susie-did-it theory in short order.

Fritz Klenner certainly didn't need Susie to find Delores Lynch's house. He knew how to read maps and how to navigate in new territory, and Prospect, Kentucky isn't Ultima Thule. Over a period of time, he could have pumped Susie for the required information, and she would have given him everything he needed without even being aware of it. He'd probably seen and memorized pictures of the house, details of Delores's daily routine, the works. It was a very skillful assassination.

There's no doubt that Susie hated Delores Lynch, hated her with all the venom she could muster — both because Delores had never liked *her*, and because Delores was helping to finance Tom's legal campaign to obtain better visitation rights with the boys. But I don't believe Susie took part in the Lynch killings.

There's a big difference between being grateful for the results of murder and actually being present when it is committed or urging its commission. That's a responsibility — the responsibility of knowing the truth — that Susie couldn't assume. And Fritz protected her from having to assume it.

No, I think my sister Susie would simply tell Fritz about her problems and her fears, and Fritz would go away somewhere and fix things for her. Then he would explain what happened with some fable that she longed to believe.

But even after Delores Lynch was "fixed," my sister's problems weren't over. For one thing, Tom Lynch inherited his mother's estate, so he was financially able to continue pressing his court efforts for better visitation rights. And in early 1985, Tom acquired new allies from another quarter — our side of the family. Our parents, concerned over Susie's erratic behavior and her relationship with Fritz Klenner, sympathized with Tom Lynch's attempts to gain more access to his sons.

A court hearing on the matter was scheduled for May 23. On May 17, our father, Robert Newsom Jr., in his overriding desire to be fair, telephoned Susie and informed her that he intended to testify on Tom Lynch's behalf at the hearing. In effect, he would be helping to make the case against his own daughter. I'm sure he made that call sadly and with all the gentleness he could command.

Susie, of course, would have told Fritz about the call immediately. All of her old fears would have been flooding over her at that point, and she probably ranted and raved about how her own people were betraying her.

I think it's likely that our father's phone call sealed his fate — and that of our mother, Florence, and grandmother, Hattie.

CHAPTER TWENTY-FOUR

How to Get Closer to God

Ian Perkins had known Fritz Klenner all his life. Both men grew up in the same small town of Reidsville. Ian's grandfather, a close friend of Doc Klenner's, had been Fritz's godfather. Ian Perkins's mother claimed that Doc had cured her of polio with his vitamin C shots (although, since it was Doc himself who made the diagnosis, nobody will ever know if she really had polio). Ian's mother and her second husband lived, for a period of time, on the same block as the Klenners. And Doc Klenner had delivered Ian Perkins into the world in 1964.

Although Ian saw Fritz regularly as he was growing up, the eleven-year difference in their ages kept them from becoming close friends until 1984. By then, Ian was majoring in philosophy at Washington and Lee University in Lexington, Virginia. An ardently patriotic young man with a bright future, Ian had had a number of discussions with Fritz about the training of a battlefield medic. Ian had received medical training in the National Guard, but Fritz promptly pointed out a number of omissions and mistakes in Perkins's curriculum. Perkins was convinced that Fritz was a real doctor.

Ian Perkins's adventures with Fritz Klenner began with a discussion between the two men during Ian's midterm break in February

1985. Fritz invited Ian up to the Klenner farm to go shooting out on Bigfoot's north forty. While Ian and Fritz cavorted around in the woods, chucking dynamite charges into holes in yet another attempt to find the elusive lava bores, they had a serious discussion about Ian's future. Ian told Fritz he was considering a career in intelligence. One of Ian's uncles had CIA connections and had promised to help get him into the screening program.

It is easy to imagine the look that came over Fritz's face when he learned this. He was probably already figuring out ways in which Ian and his naive passion for professional spookery could be useful. So Ian wanted to work for the Agency? Well, Fritz could dig it. In fact, he confided to Perkins, he himself had been doing work for the Agency since college. The details were classified, of course, but he could tell Ian that he had participated in a number of dangerous covert operations. He had had to take lives on some of them and had even come close to being killed on several occasions.

"These experiences," he assured Ian, "have brought me closer to God."

Anxious to get closer to God himself, Perkins didn't bat an eye when Fritz later offered him a small supporting role as the getaway driver and back-up man in an upcoming mission. The job? To take out a KGB-connected drug smuggler who lived on the outskirts of Winston-Salem. Fritz needed a steady man to back him up. Did Perkins have the kidney for it? If so, his future with The Company could be bright indeed. Gosh, thought Ian, what a lucky break!

Fritz concocted an elaborate ruse to establish their alibi: a weekend camping trip to the Peaks of Otter in Virginia. By reserving a site there and setting up camp, they would have an almost-foolproof alibi, since they obviously couldn't be in two places at once. The reserved campsite receipt would be documentary evidence that they were at Peaks of Otter when the hit took place in Winston-Salem. Of course, they probably wouldn't even need an alibi, but they'd have one just in case.

On Saturday, May 18, 1985, Fritz and Ian began their CIA mission. They drove to Virginia, set up camp at Peaks of Otter, then stealthily abandoned their campsite and drove south. By 11 p.m. they had arrived at the outskirts of Winston-Salem. Ian parked the Blazer, and Fritz stepped out of the car and into the night, dressed and armed for a clandestine operation. Ian drove away as Fritz headed into the darkness.

Four blocks away, at 3239 Valley Road in the Winston-Salem suburb of Old Town, three people were sitting up watching TV: Hattie "Nana" Newsom, Susie's 85-year-old grandmother, and Susie's parents, 65-year-old Robert Newsom Jr. and 66-year-old Florence Newsom. It was a typical Saturday evening at Hattie's big, white house. Bob and Florence customarily spent their weekends with Hattie, and they were looking forward to moving in with her as soon as the remodeling on the house was completed.

As the TV droned on, Hattie began drifting off to sleep on the couch. Florence was snacking on some grapes. Outside, it was dark and still. In fact, the Old Town neighborhood was generally so peaceful at night that the Newsoms rarely bothered to lock their door.

CHAPTER TWENTY-FIVE

The Second Mission
Old Town, N.C., May 18, 1985

Time: 2300 hours. The chain-link fence is child's play. Now that he is moving in the darkness under the trees, across this expansive, isolated, set-back yard, there is little chance of anyone seeing him. He is a raven's shadow crossing the lawn, at one with the night.

His excitement has been building since he left the mountains late that afternoon, building with each buzzing spin of the Blazer's oversized tires. He feels even better than he did that morning in Kentucky. Acutely conscious of every cricket's chirp and frog's croak, and of the distant whisper of traffic on Reynolda Road, he edges closer to the big white house.

He is wearing a bulletproof vest. The old man is supposed to be a pacifist, but out here in the country it's just possible he might keep a shotgun around. Besides, it's a nice touch to help convince Ian of the seriousness of this mission. He wears a windbreaker over the vest and surgical gloves on his hands. In the padded, lightweight case he's carrying is a .22-caliber pistol, a competition-quality .45-caliber automatic, some spare clips of ammo, and a bayonet. Tools of the trade, and quality tools, every one.

His main worry is the time. His habit of driving cautiously to every destination sometimes makes it hard to gauge arrival times, and he is arriving a bit later than would be ideal. It's after eleven, and none of his targets is a night owl. Still, he knows that sometimes they do stay up later on Saturday night.

115

Now he's close enough to see that the lights are still on in the living room and to hear the faint sound of a TV. He moves carefully around the side of the garage and checks out the cars. The grandmother's keys, he discovers, are still in the ignition of the gold-colored Plymouth. That's the one he'll have to take, although it isn't much of a vehicle. He sidles around the far side of the parking area and enters a breezeway through a screen door that he knows is never locked.

Even before this second mission is completed, he is already looking forward to the third and final mission, the one in New Mexico, where he will stalk and happily kill the dentist. Susie told him what a bad person the dentist is, and Susie wouldn't lie. That guy is bound to be into drugs. Besides, he's two-timing Susie, and clearly he does not deserve to ever see his two boys again. In fact, the dentist probably deserves to die more than these old folks here tonight, but first things first. And later, once the dentist, too, is gone, their way will be clear, and they can take the money Susie will inherit (a tidy sum, she says) and make serious preparations for The End.

The imminence of The End calms him. That's one reason why he feels so detached from the moral dimensions of what he is about to do. In three or four years, all of these people are going to be blown away in the great catastrophe anyway. All he's doing tonight, and for that matter all he did in Kentucky, was to slightly advance the timetable.

He peers now through the window in the door that leads from the breezeway to the living room. His unknowing targets are all cozy and drowsy in their chairs. The old lady is munching grapes from a bowl on a table by her chair. The granny is dozing on the sofa. They all have the look of people who are just about ready to call it a night.

It's going to be fun doing in the old lady. She has said things to him that nobody had ever dared say before, calling him a fraud and an immoral liar. "You're even crazier than your father!" she had blurted out at one point. That remark, even though it was made months and months ago, sealed her fate. Her and all her kind! All those years of laughing at the Klenners, all those nasty little Catholic-baiting cracks about his father's beliefs. Didn't they see what a saint his father was? No, more than that, what a demigod, what a great and glorious healer, his father had been? How could they say anything bad against him? How could they expect to say the things they had said and not suffer his vengeance for it? He will take a special pleasure from putting a touch on the old woman.

As for the old man, what kind of a louse would go to court and testify against his own daughter? Taking sides with the dentist against Susie! He doesn't deserve to have such a daughter, and for betraying her, he deserves to die. He has no feelings about the granny-lady one way or the other. She's not important except as a witness, somebody in the wrong place at the wrong time.

Kneeling, he takes the .45 out of the case, pushes back the slide, and lets it ride home, heavy with its blunt, thick cartridge. Safety off. Whispers of steel and brass.

He plans to open the door silently, and just suddenly *be there*. Sudden Death come out of the night. They will freeze at the sight, he hopes. He has a few things to say to them, while he has them there as a captive audience. It is not enough for them to die. They must also be told why, must hear, listen as their sins are read from his lips. The aesthetics of the act, the fineness of the moral equation he's worked out, demand that they know.

The old lady bends over for another grape, her bony shoulders rising toward him. Just that quickly, he changes tactics. After all, death explained is measurably less malign than death irrational and motiveless. Does God ever tell you why before He does it? Out of his detestation for the old lady, he decides that even a single word of explanation would be too much mercy. But a quick pistol shot would be merciful, too. He decides to knife her first, then shoot her. Cold steel for the first blow, then the gun. The timing will be tricky, a virtuoso stunt really, but he has the skills to do it.

He reaches back into his case and takes out the bayonet, shifting the .45 to his belt. He curls his latex-covered fingers around the doorknob and turns it soundlessly, as smoothly as a good surgeon making the first cut. The door opens. They look up and recognize him.

The old lady is still halfway to the grape bowl when he reaches for her and whips the bayonet down in two quick, shallow, slicing cuts to the neck. Then he raises the blade with more deliberation and drives it deep into her right shoulder. As she screams in pain, he decides to leave it stuck there.

Now the solid, checkered heft of the pistol's grip fills his hand. Across the room, the old man is rising in a desperate attempt to defend his bleeding wife. He looks like someone swimming through heavy surf. Horrified and astonished, he can only exclaim with a round-mouthed "Ooooh!" as he starts to lurch forward.

The killer indulges in the luxury of a calm, two-fisted combat shooting stance. The bore of the .45 must look like a railroad tunnel to the old man, for now he tries to check his forward motion, and instinctively throws up his arms in feeble self-protection.

The first shot is shockingly loud in the close confines of the room. It smashes through part of the old man's right forearm before drilling into his abdomen — a messy hit that flings pieces of bone about the room. Howling, the old man is thrown back by the impact. The Agent braces against the recoil and fires two more rounds. The angles of penetration change between rounds as the heavy slugs hit the old man's body. The last shot, which enters beneath the rib cage, bores into his heart and punches him all the way back through the archway that leads to the foyer.

Over on the sofa, Granny is waking up, her eyes rolling with incomprehension. The Agent swings around. His first shot grazes her temple, throwing her back down against the sofa. The second shot strikes her low, on the side, and she sinks back into the cushions. He crosses the room and puts the coup de grace round into her temple. The stick-thin body goes still and she looks peaceful, even with that messy entrance wound facing him like a wet red eye.

Near his feet, the old lady with the bayonet in her shoulder is struggling to her knees. She wants to go out fighting. Even now, she is groping for a long, brass-tipped andiron sticking up from a stand of fireplace tools. It's the only thing in the room that could be used as a weapon. He steps back to take aim, kicking over a rocking chair that blocks his path. The old woman gropes for the fireplace tools, misses them, sends them sprawling in a brassy clatter. He drops her with one shot to the chest.

Calmly, he slaps a fresh magazine into the butt of the .45 and crosses the room to the foyer. He pumps one final, just-to-make-sure round into the old man's head. Giddy with his success, the Agent humors himself for just a moment and walks back over to the sofa. He rearranges Granny — a devout Moravian and Sunday school teacher — into an attitude of prayer, hands folded. For the finishing touch, he drapes her snugly with the multicolored afghan he finds on the back of the sofa.

While contemplating his craftsmanship, a sudden noise makes him spin around. The old lady, some flutter of vitality still pumping away in her flayed body, is moving again. He comes close to her. He wants her to look up and see this final round coming, but she doesn't understand what he's saying. Even after he fires that last round into her skull, she still seems tauntingly alive. Suddenly he is overcome by a moment of sweet, hot rage. Pay-back time, old woman. Yanking out the bayonet still lodged in her shoulder, he jumps onto her corpse and plunges the bayonet repeatedly into the middle of her back, his anger growing with each stab. How satisfyingly the flesh parts for his blade!

Then he pulls the melon-heavy head back and cuts her taut, white throat. He has read Ninja legends about the poetic sound of blood rushing through a certain kind of throat-cut. Great swordsmen have written delicate haiku about that rare nuance of their art. He, though, evidently lacks the necessary finesse, because all he hears is the sad, damp sigh of collapsing organs and traumatized tissue.

He glances at his watch, a heavy, stainless-steel Rolex. 2330 hours. Time to clean up. He places both the bayonet and the pistol back in their case. Then he methodically polices the room for his spent brass, knowing that a fired shell casing bears marks as peculiar to the gun that fired it as his fingerprints are to his hand. He knows exactly how many shots he fired and he knows roughly where the ejected brass must have landed. In the living room he finds all except one of the casings. Try as he might, he cannot find the one that flew from the gun when he administered the coup de grace to the old man in the hallway.

Now he begins to doubt his own arithmetic. Has he miscounted his shots, or has he really lost a shell casing? Miscounting would be stupid and unprofessional, but *losing* one is potentially a serious problem. Did the casing fall down a heating duct? Is the old man lying on top of it? Has the Agent himself kicked it into some unseen crevice?

Time is beginning to move faster now. Someone may have heard the shots. A .45 makes a real lease-breaker of a bang. He needs to get into the car, get away, and make his rendezvous with Ian. He doesn't have any more time to search for the missing casing. If he is late, Ian may get spooked and that could mean problems.

He goes back through the living room, which is now reeking with powder. Carefully avoiding the stickiness on the rug, he exits through the breezeway. Outside, he gulps the fragrant, late-spring air of the night. The neighborhood looks quiet. Mission accomplished.

CHAPTER TWENTY-SIX

Covering Tracks

Nervous but exhilarated, Ian Perkins whiled away the time at a nearby Burger King after dropping off Fritz for his CIA mission against the KGB-connected drug smugglers. Then he drove Fritz's Blazer back to the rendezvous point, arriving about midnight.

Part of the plan called for Fritz to steal a car at the site of his job, then drive it to Charlotte for another hit. (The identity of this target is unclear; this entire aspect of the plan, in fact, may have been a deliberate obfuscation on Fritz's part.) So Ian was not startled to see Fritz arriving in a gold-colored Plymouth. Falling in behind the Plymouth, Ian followed Fritz for a couple of miles down University Parkway, near the campus of Wake Forest University in Winston-Salem. Fritz was driving very slowly and deliberately, as always.

Suddenly, out of the darkness, a police car appeared. Blue lights flashing, the cruiser interposed itself between Ian and Fritz. Ian, trying not to reveal his sudden apprehension, drove the Blazer out and around the other two vehicles as Fritz pulled obediently to the shoulder. The officer ignored the Blazer as Ian drove it away, pulling up instead behind Fritz in the gold-colored Plymouth.

Inside the Plymouth, Fritz calmly snuggled his .45-caliber automatic under his coat, aiming it toward the door. If the patrolman asked him to step out of the car, Fritz was ready to kill him on the spot.

Winston-Salem police officer James Hull knew nothing of what had just transpired at Hattie Newsom's home on Valley Road that night. He had stopped Fritz merely because he thought it a bit peculiar for someone to be driving so slowly, along a major thoroughfare, at that late hour. Intoxicated drivers, he knew, sometimes drove with the same exaggerated caution. But Fritz seemed quite sober as the officer questioned him. He was cooperative and calm, and the check went off without a hitch. Fritz explained that he was having car trouble. The Plymouth was just not accelerating like it ought to and he would have it looked at soon. It was a plausible story, and it satisfied the officer. He didn't even ask Fritz to step out of the car. Hull bade Fritz a good evening and included the incident, without further comment, in his routine report.

A short distance up the road, Ian had parked the Blazer at another Burger King where Fritz couldn't possibly miss it. Ian went inside for coffee while he waited for Fritz. Fritz arrived shortly, looking remarkably unruffled. He'd bluffed his way through it. No big deal. Easy as pie. But there were problems with the gold Plymouth, Fritz explained. Perhaps he realized, for the first time, what a dumb thing he had done by stealing a murdered woman's car and then running into a conscientious policeman on his way back from the scene of the crime. Fritz told Ian that the car was no good, and that the Charlotte half of the mission would have to be scrubbed.

Ian followed Fritz back to the original drop-off location near Valley Road and waited in the shadows for him to return. After a while, Fritz returned on foot. Then they headed back to Virginia in Fritz's Blazer. At a curb market in Mount Airy, North Carolina, Fritz tore up his shirt, shoes, and hat, hacking at them with a big survival knife until they were in tatters. Then he wadded them up and chucked them into a dumpster, along with the foam padding from inside his gun case. A bit later, at a rest stop on Interstate 77, Fritz shaved off his beard.

Once they were back in the mountains, Fritz removed the barrel from his .45 and threw it into a lake. This insured that ballistics tests could not link the spent slugs to his weapon. He also trashed his windbreaker and gun case, and buried his bayonet in some woods just off the Blue Ridge Parkway. Later, Fritz would polish the gun's extractor with a small grinding wheel. This polishing, called "jewelling," makes an extractor function more smoothly and imparts an attractive finish to the metal. It has the additional effect of making it impossible for forensic tests to ever link it to a spent shell casing fired previously from that particular gun.

After the two young men returned to the safety of their campsite at Peaks of Otter in Virginia, both got sick to their stomachs.

Was the mission that rough? Ian asked Fritz.

Pretty hairy, Fritz admitted. He was forced to knife two security guards before he could kill the drug dealer.

The Kind of Man My Father Was

I want to tell you a little story about my father, Robert Newsom Jr., who died alongside my mother, Florence, and grandmother, Hattie, on that terrible night in May 1985. My father weathered a trying personal crisis fairly late in his life, and what happened to him is worth telling because it illustrates why I will always think of him as a good and honorable man.

He was a company man. He first went to work for R.J. Reynolds in 1945 and stayed with them until 1968, when he moved over to the food division of Reynolds Industries and went to live in Connecticut. But he missed the tobacco business, missed living in North Carolina, and detested several of his new supervisors. So, after a couple of years working in New York for Reynolds, he joined Lorillard, another tobacco company, and moved back to Greensboro.

When Lorillard was later acquired by new owners, they hired as their chief executive a man who had been a tobacco executive for Reynolds. He hired my father as director of engineering for Lorillard, and was grooming him for the job of chief operations officer.

In 1974, the clerical workers at Lorillard began to talk about forming a union. To head off this move, my father spoke to them at a mass meeting — his remarks having been cleared with the management's labor lawyers — and outlined the following company position. He could assure them that, if they did not go union, they would all continue to enjoy full employment, the number of positions would remain the same, there wouldn't be any restructuring of the clerical staff, and there would be no retaliatory firings against the people who had been lobbying for a union.

Largely as a result of my father's speech, the union was not voted in, much to the joy of Lorillard management. Not long after that, my father's superior, the man who had hired him, called him into his office and handed him a list of names. These people would have to be fired because of their pro-union activities. Would my father please take care of it?

My father stated that to do so would make both the corporation, and himself, into liars. Furthermore, it was his opinion that such draconian action would only rekindle pro-union feelings, sow the seeds of distrust with regard to any future management policies, and would, in short, play right into the hands of the union. Firing these people, he continued, would do severe harm to employee morale, would damage productivity, and would probably be considered an unfair labor practice, should any of the fired men seek legal restitution — as some of them surely would.

My father was then given three choices: proceed as ordered, resign, or be fired. He resigned. He had given his word to those people that no one would lose their job because of the union referendum, and he would not permit himself to be made into a liar.

I think it's significant that, when he was asked why my father had left Lorillard, his superior stated: "He was too nice a man to be an operations officer for a major corporation." In other words, he was not a liar or a thief.

A goodly number of people were sacked from their jobs not long after my father left, but there are still wage-and-hour employees at Lorillard who remember him well because of what he did.

I tell this story not to nominate my father for posthumous sainthood, but simply to illustrate the fact that in all my life, I never knew him to do a dishonest or a dishonorable thing. When a man like that is killed, the whole world loses something.

CHAPTER TWENTY-EIGHT

Discoveries

On Saturday, May 18, 1985, Robert Newsom Jr. and his wife Florence had gone to Old Town near Winston-Salem to visit Bob's 85-year-old mother, Hattie "Nana" Newsom. It had become a normal part of their routine to spend their weekends with Hattie; they planned to move in with her as soon as the remodeling to her house at 3239 Valley Road was finished. On Sunday, May 19, Robert and Florence were supposed to pick up their granddaughter, Page, from the home of her other grandparents and bring her back home to Greensboro.

At about five o'clock on Sunday afternoon, Page called her parents, Robert and Alice Newsom III, to say that Bob and Florence hadn't yet come by. What should she do? Alice Newsom told her mother to let Page stay for supper while Alice tried to find out what was delaying Bob and Florence. She immediately called Hattie's house in Old Town, and grew uneasy when there was no answer. Robert III then tried several Greensboro numbers, including his father's office, on the off-chance that Bob and Florence had simply forgotten about Page or that Bob had been called back to work for some extraordinary reason. Nothing.

Alice's parents took Page to a favorite eatery in Kernersville, a little town halfway between Greensboro and Winston-Salem. Alice and Robert III drove over and picked up their daughter, then went back to Greensboro and tried to resume their normal Sunday night TV-watching. However, when they still hadn't heard from Bob and Florence by ten o'clock, Robert III decided to drive over to Hattie's and check things out personally.

Then Alice had a better idea. Why not call Hattie's doctor, Homer Sutton, who lived closer to Hattie, and ask him to go by and check? Doctor Sutton was in bed, reading, when Robert III called. Nevertheless, he was more than willing to check up on Hattie Newsom. She had been his patient for 30 years and he cared for her deeply. His wife, Kattie, agreed to accompany him to the Newsom residence.

It was about 10:30 Sunday evening when the Suttons arrived. Doctor Sutton glanced at the driveway and recognized Bob and Florence Newsom's car, as well as the vehicles that belonged to Hattie — both of them Plymouths, one of them gold-colored. The house was disconcertingly quiet and Bob's car shouldn't have been there that late. The Suttons headed for the back door, the one habitually used by friends and family alike. Doctor Sutton saw the broken storm-door glass. His apprehension growing, he peered through the window into the living room, where the TV set was on and the lights were burning.

The first person he saw was Hattie, in an attitude of prayerful sleep on the sofa, covered with her favorite afghan. Then he spotted Florence, on the floor, in a position that she might have adopted while watching TV. Except that Florence, at her age, did not normally flop out on the floor like a teenager. The incongruity of the scene made him peer more closely.

Then he saw the blood. Those two people, he realized, were dead. From the look of it, murdered. He could not see Bob from where he was standing. Then Sutton realized that the killer might still be in the house. Prudently, the Suttons withdrew to a neighbor's house and called the police. Then they called their son and asked him to notify Robert Newsom III in Greensboro.

The Suttons, along with a neighbor and Hattie Newsom's pastor, took up a vigil at the end of the Newsom driveway. Thirty minutes after the 911 emergency call was made, a police car arrived. The officer entered the Newsom home, found Bob Newsom Jr.'s bullet-ridden body in the hallway, and verified that all three Newsoms were dead: Bob, Florence, and Hattie.

The crime scene was gruesome, with blood splattered everywhere. Whoever had killed these defenseless people had made sure they were dead by firing a final heavy-caliber shot into each victim's head at point-blank range. Then, coldly, the killer had paused to fold Hattie Newsom's hands in mock prayer. And Florence Newsom had been sadistically hacked up with a knife.

Curiously, there was also a burned spot, about a yard wide, close to Bob Newsom's feet in the hall. Some papers from a nearby drawer and, on closer inspection, from Bob's briefcase, had obviously been used to kindle the fire, but it had burned itself out before igniting anything else.

Aside from the charred papers, and the signs of struggle in the living room, nothing appeared to have been disturbed. There were plenty of valuables in plain sight that had not been touched. There was entry damage to the storm door, which made it look like a robbery, and the murders could have been a classic case of a desperate burglar caught in the act and shooting his way out in a panic. But professional robbers, and most savvy amateurs as well, are not stupid enough to break into a house where there are three clearly visible people at home, still awake, watching TV. And the murders seemed so deliberate. All things considered, Hattie Newsom's home did not look like it had been visited by a thief. It looked more like a squad of terrorists had targeted the place for a vengeance raid.

The Winston-Salem police were first on the scene, and they quickly cordoned off the property. Then somebody remembered that this area of Old Town had not yet been incorporated into the city of Winston-Salem. Therefore, the case fell under the jurisdiction of the Forsyth County Sheriff's Department. This was the first of several confusions that would characterize the way the case was handled by the authorities.

Assigned to manage the case was Sergeant Allen Gentry, a 32-year-old career detective with a keen mind. After inspecting the scene, Gentry requested help from the State Bureau of Investigation. The SBI agent assigned to help Gentry was Tom Sturgill, with whom he had worked several times before. Meanwhile, a stunned Robert Newsom III had arrived from Greensboro. Gentry felt for the man and treated him gently, asking him only a basic minimum of questions before sending him home.

On the way back to Greensboro, riding with a friend who had offered to stand by him on that lonely night, Robert Newsom III suddenly realized who had murdered his family.

CHAPTER TWENTY-NINE

Funeral Rites

Detective Gentry spent all of Sunday night at the scene of the Newsom killings on Valley Road, poking around. The SBI's mobile crime lab arrived shortly before dawn and its crew of technicians began their arcane studies. Also arriving at about that time was Forsyth County District Attorney Don Tisdale.

The D.A. was there at such an ungodly hour because these slaughtered people were not vagrants knifed in an alleyway; they were community leaders, widely known and cared about in their hometown. The media coverage was bound to be intense, and the heat would be on for the investigators to come up with something tangible, real fast.

The first order of business was to question the neighbors and the construction workers who had been remodeling the house. This was time-consuming and, in the end, produced nothing. Not a hint.

Next the investigation focused on Tom and Susie Lynch's custody battle. Here, at least, was a family squabble acrimonious enough to warrant closer study. As Gentry pored over a pile of legal documents, one fact leaped out at him that confirmed something he had learned Sunday night: Bob Newsom Jr. had been scheduled to testify against his own daughter's case only a few days after he was murdered.

On Tuesday, Gentry telephoned Tom Lynch in New Mexico. Gentry learned more about the connection between the Newsom family and the murders of Delores and Jane Lynch in Kentucky. He also learned of Tom's suspicion that the common link between the two vicious crimes was Susie's weird cousin, Fritz Klenner.

As for Susie, well, the other members of the family became increasingly aware that something was not right about her reaction to the Valley Road horrors. Alice Newsom, Susie's sister-in-law, was among the first to wonder about Susie. When Susie had first been notified, late Sunday night, that there had been an "accident" at Hattie's house, she responded without alarm or even concern. And when Alice Newsom later called to confirm that Susie's mother, father, and grandmother were all murdered, Susie didn't burst into tears as Alice expected. Instead, Susie merely responded in a flat, hollow voice: "Well…there's nothing left, is there?"

Alice offered to arrange for someone to come and stay with Susie, but Susie declined. One of her chow dogs had run off, she said, and she had to go out looking for him — expressing, Alice thought, more concern about the animal than about the death of her own parents and grandmother.

By this time, Susie rarely communicated with her old friends, and when she did, it was usually on her terms and with strange motives. On the day of the murders, for instance, she had spent some time with a woman named Annette Hunt, though whether or not she was consciously attempting to establish an alibi remains a matter of conjecture.

When Annette Hunt heard about the tragedy in Old Town, she went over to Susie's apartment and tried to comfort her. Susie was subdued, but hardly grief-stricken. The two boys were in school, just like any other day, and Susie said she had not yet broken the news to them. The two women had tea together. Ms. Hunt inquired about Fritz. Fritz was asleep, Susie told her. He'd been up all night hunting for a missing chow dog.

The Newsom funerals were scheduled for Thursday, May 23, 1985. On Tuesday, while Susie and her brother Robert Newsom III were in Winston-Salem finalizing the arrangements, Fritz took the two boys over to Annette Hunt's for the day. After Susie returned from Winston-Salem, she spent some time at Bob III's house in Greensboro. Ms. Hunt offered to take Susie and the boys back to their Friendly Hills apartment and help Susie with some of her domestic chores.

Just after the two women had finished walking the dogs, Fritz burst into the apartment in a rage. How dare Susie go out at night alone! Didn't she realize the danger they were all in? She should never, ever, go *anywhere* without letting him know! Susie accepted his tantrum meekly.

Detective Gentry had meanwhile tried, several times, to get in touch with Susie. He tried all the more urgently, now that he knew details about the legal battle over the children. When he tried unsuccessfully to reach her by phone on Monday, he drove to the Friendly Hills apartment and left his card in the door. He finally spoke to her by phone on Tuesday. Susie seemed remarkably indifferent to his request for an interview. She had lots of other stuff to do, she said; maybe she could see him tomorrow, maybe at ten in the morning.

Gentry was starting to feel disturbances in the air whenever he focused on Susie and Fritz. Susie's parents and grandmother have just been brutally murdered, and when he calls up and asks for help in the investigation, she says she has *other stuff to do?*

Bob and Florence Newsom's funeral was at ten a.m. Thursday at St. Paul's Church in Winston-Salem. Susie, Fritz, and the two boys came into the chapel through the back door. Susie had seen the press photographers waiting outside the church, and that seemed to spook her. There could be kidnappers lurking in that crowd, posing as reporters, she told one of the people who helped them to their seats.

Hattie "Nana" Newsom's funeral was held an hour later, at Bethabara Moravian Church in Winston-Salem. Then, at noon, there was a graveside service for all three victims. All told, it was a very somber morning for the survivors and friends of the shattered family. But Susie's reaction was one of remarkable stoicism. It did not go unnoticed that she went through the entire morning dry-eyed, while everybody else desperately supported each other on the edge of emotional collapse. Fritz Klenner stayed at the rear of the crowd, minding the boys, throughout the graveside ceremonies.

Several people who talked with Susie at the family gathering afterward noticed that she seemed curiously free of grief. Rather than talk about her parents, she ranted angrily to anyone who would listen about some statements in the morning paper by Forsyth County Sheriff Preston Oldham, in which he drew some parallels between the Newsom killings in Old Town and the still-unsolved Lynch murders in Kentucky. Susie was infuriated. "The nerve of him!" she hissed.

Future Generations

It is possible that, by the time our parents were killed, Susie was so far gone into fantasyland that she may have come to believe something truly horrible: that if her children could not be raised in accordance with her new view of reality, then it was better that they not live at all.

Of course, none of us knew about the whole Armageddon thing until much later, but I remember vividly something that happened on the day after my parents' funeral, when we were taking inventory of some family possessions. Mother had some fine jewelry, and we offered some to Susie. We told her the rings would be great for John and Jim to give to their fiancees some day, something that would mean a lot both to the boys and to their intended brides.

"No," said Susie, "My sons will never marry." She gave her head a small shake, qualifying the remark sadly, a little wistfully: "Not after what they've seen of my marriage."

CHAPTER THIRTY-ONE

La Folie a Deux

It is certain my Conviction gains infinitely, the moment another soul will believe in it.

— "Novalis" (Baron Freidrich von Hardenburg, 1772-1801)

There is a name for what was happening between Fritz Klenner and Susie Newsom Lynch, and it sends at least some beam of light into the dark psychic caves of their behavior.

Because it is impossible to know what motivated Fritz's final, most desperate actions, large areas of their relationship will forever remain mysterious. But some degree of comprehension, the beginnings of understanding at least, comes from the knowledge that the nature of their relationship has a clinical name, recognized symptoms, and its own branch of psychiatric literature.

The relationship between Susie and Fritz was like a double spiral of DNA. Their mutual needs, fears, insecurities, paranoias, and aggressions fit like protein molecules snuggling into their templates. In time, with pressure from outside realities — realities whose authority over any aspect of their lives neither person could acknowledge — the spiral overtightened.

The pressures on them intensified their psychotic tendencies to the bursting point. Fritz was doubtless already over the edge into delusional paranoia before he took up with Susie, but he didn't start killing people until after the two of them had bonded together. Two borderline psychotics came together, and together, they generated a

137

state of delusion significantly stronger and more dangerous than that from which they suffered singly.

The name for this condition is *la folie a deux* ("madness between two"). You won't find this syndrome listed in most college textbooks on psychiatry. It is too rare. Most practicing psychiatrists go through their entire careers without encountering a single bonafide case.

The medical literature on the syndrome is not exhaustive. Unlike, say, schizophrenia, whose bibliography alone would fill a volume the size of an unabridged dictionary, the literature on *la folie a deux* can be listed on perhaps four or five pages.

La folie a deux received its name, and its first detailed clinical description, a century ago in the writings of two pioneering psychiatrists named Falret and Lasegue. (Their original work, published in 1877, was reprinted in 1964 in the *American Journal of Psychiatry*, 121:1.) Subsequent writers have attempted to coin other names for it ("infectious insanity," "psychic infection," "contagious insanity," "reciprocal insanity," "psychosis of association," "double insanity," "conjugal insanity," "influenced psychosis," and even "mystic paranoia"), but none covers it as well, or with as much cachet, as the original.

Under normal circumstances, of course, mental illness is never contagious in the same sense as diseases borne by bacteria or viruses. Rather, *la folie a deux* is a mutual amplification of two existing mental illnesses. As Falret and Lasegue wrote: "In 'folie a deux,' one individual is the active element...he creates the delusion and gradually imposes it upon the second, or passive, one; little by little the latter resists the pressure of his associate, continuously reacting to correct, modify, and coordinate the delusional material. The delusion soon becomes their common cause, to be repeated to all in almost identical fashion."

In their description of the circumstances in which the syndrome can flourish, Lasegue and Falret give an uncannily accurate account of the circumstances in which Fritz and Susie lived during 1984 and 1985:

"To allow this intellectual process to take place in two different minds, it is necessary for both individuals to have lived a very close-knit existence in the same environment for a long period of time, sharing the same feelings, the same interests, the same apprehensions and the same hopes, and be completely isolated from any outside influences...The delusion should be kept within the bounds of the possible, based on past events, an apprehension or hope in the future. This condition of probability itself makes it communicable from one individual to another and allows the conviction of one to take root in the mind of the other."

For a psychiatrist to diagnose a case of *la folie a deux*, then, three conditions must be present:

The content, scope, and motifs of the delusional ideas must be identical in both partners;

There must be definite evidence that both partners are, and have been for some time, intimately associated;

There must be evidence that both partners share, unquestioningly accept, and constantly support each other's delusions.

The incidence of *la folie a deux* seems highest among people who belong to the same family. Mother/daughter relationships seem to outweigh all others, but it is also common between spouses as well as in the less close relationships within a family — cousins, for instance. It is thought, therefore, that some obscure set of hereditary factors may predispose certain individuals toward this condition. Simple intimacy may be enough, however, to trigger the syndrome.

For *la folie a deux* to occur, the two individuals must enter into an exceptional kind of relationship. One of the two individuals is the dominant partner. He is usually the more intelligent, although one may substitute "more willful" or "more powerful" for "more intelligent." This person persistently and gradually imposes his delusions on the more passive and originally healthy partner.

The two individuals must live together in a very hermetic environment, their daily routines closely knit, for a relatively long period of time. The greater their isolation from the outside world, the quicker the syndrome takes root and the faster it flourishes.

The delusions shared between these people are usually not completely impossible. They are kept (though often just barely) within the realm of the possible. The basis for the delusions may be past

139

events, or shared expectations for the future.

An excellent example of *la folie a deux* is reported by Doctors Robert and Kay Faguet (Department of Psychiatry, University of California at Los Angeles, in Friedmann and Fageut: *Extraordinary Disorders of Human Behavior*, Plenum Press, New York, 1982). This is a mother-daughter case in which the mother became convinced not only that unexplained acts of mayhem were taking place in the neighborhood, but also that unidentified parties were attempting to poison them by flooding their residence with pesticides.

The Faguets reproduce a letter, jointly written by the two patients. Here are some excerpts:

> Dear Doctor: ...There is much to tell you about us — not too good. I'm afraid our neighbor, Mr. N., ...was murdered Christmas Eve by a man who entered his home through a hole they had made in his roof, robbed him and attacked him. Now it is thought advisable for us to have an armed guard. Also, something is pumped into our living room. It collects on beams, wooded furniture, a large tray etc. We sent a specimen to H...and the report came back that our specimen consisted of eighteen different pesticides. We are told that those with criminal intent are trying to drive us out of our house! We keep getting offers for it, but we are not ready to leave yet...Enclosed is a copy, Xerox, of the lab report about the stuff being pumped into our living room. The stuff looks just like mildew on the ceiling beams, furniture, the tray and other things. That's what people thought it was until this report came. It's damaged our dog's pancreas...and sometimes we feel sick. We're awfully glad to have this evidence and not be thought paranoid any more.

To back up their claim, they submitted to their doctor a copy of the chemical analysis they had concocted of a "Kleenex wipe taken from tray in living room." A methodical and detailed document, it lists nineteen different kinds of toxic chemicals, from paraquat to DDT, and gives the measurements of particles found of each.

Fritz Klenner's *Time* photograph was documentation of the same sort.

Here is an interesting description of the personal dynamic at work in a *la folie a deux* relationship (Lehmann, p. 726):

> The primary focus of induced psychosis is usually a paranoid or paraphrenic schizophrenic whose special adjustment to the world is characterized not only by his persecutory and grandiose delusions but also by a deeply rooted relationship with another person, who is usually in the dependent position. The recipient or passive partner in this psychotic relationship has much in common with the dominant partner because of many shared life experiences, common needs and hopes, and, most importantly, a deep emotional rapport with and concern for the partner. In order to relinquish his contact with reality to the extent of sharing the delusions of the other person, he must probably be very restricted in his ability to form relationships with other people. He is then faced with the choice of either losing the only person to whom he has been — and perhaps ever will be — very close, or joining that person in his pathological world in order to avoid the loss. Because of the strong emotional involvement, the folie a deux psychosis has been referred to as a transference phenomenon.

The process of transferring delusions from one person to another is similar to the process of "brainwashing." In the first stage, the psychological defenses of the passive partner break down through literal and ideational isolation. The second stage is characterized by identification with the dominant person, who is often viewed by his victim as a rescuer, a vehicle for salvation. In the final stage, new ideas can be introduced, indoctrination accomplished, in an atmosphere of relative submission.

Fritz Klenner and Susie Newsom Lynch seem to fit all major points. First of all, Fritz appeared to be the dominant party in the relationship. Although it is true that Fritz was not overwhelmingly more intelligent than Susie, he was certainly a virtuoso manipulator whose relationships with women were characterized by shrewd and subtle domination games.

When Fritz and Susie were first getting reacquainted at Doc Klenner's clinic, Susie was recovering from the combined effects of a traumatic marital breakup, her failed odyssey to the Far East, and an alleged case of multiple sclerosis. She had become disengaged from life outside of her own problems, her energy level was low, she was filled with smoldering anger, and she had lost the certainties that had sustained her for years. Fritz knew how to listen, how to draw people out until he learned all their weaknesses. It would not have taken him long to figure out how to mold her to meet his needs.

As the shared madness escalated, the give-and-take between Fritz and Susie became full of loops and feedback circuits. It becomes impossible, in many instances, to figure out who was infecting whom. Still, in the minds of those who observed the process, it seems clear that Fritz was calling the shots, deciding when to turn up the psychic heat another notch. Many of the most dramatic, and all of the sickest, things that happened — the mutilation of the stuffed animals, the dramatic telephone threats — were ploys initiated by Fritz alone.

Isolation from the outside world was another critical component of their relationship. By the time of the Newsom murders in Old Town, "the world" for these two people had shrunk to the four walls of their apartment and the inside of Fritz's Blazer. Susie still permitted her sons to go to school, and with the greatest reluctance, to visit their father in New Mexico, because legally she *had* to allow these things. But otherwise, their contact with the outside world was nil. Susie had occasional visits with old friends, but they were usually strained. There was only minimal input from family members on the Newsom-Sharp side of the clan.

Contact with neighbors at the Friendly Hills apartment complex was minimal, too. Their fortress mentality is reflected in the way Fritz had the apartment decorated: the camouflage sheets hung over the windows; supplies, weapons, and camping gear heaped everywhere; the door booby-trapped with tear gas. The apartment embodied, on a small and private scale, the whole survivalist fantasy of isolation in a safe, defensible, remote locality.

Although Fritz and Susie lived in a self-created world, their delusions were still grounded, however tenuously, in "the possible." All of Fritz's survivalist scenarios were responses to atomic war, economic collapse, or natural catastrophe. As for Susie's more personal, related delusions, it was one thing to believe that Tom Lynch hobnobbed with KGB agents and Colombian drug dealers. It would have been a quite different kind of delusion, and probably a less dangerous one, to believe that Tom Lynch was actually a tentacled monster from Sirius VII who clouded people's minds with a telepathic ray gun. The former scenario, however grotesque and even laughable when held up against the objective evidence, is still, just barely, within the realm of the "possible." The latter, palpably, is not.

Fritz further broke down her old thought processes by convincing her to believe first the small lies about her ex-husband, about whom she was already inclined to believe the worst, and then the larger lies about more vast conspiracies. Once he had her sufficiently terrified, he positioned himself between her and the threats he had conjured up in the first place. He interposed his expertise as a mercenary, his arsenal of weapons, his "inside contacts," as protective barriers between Susie and her boys, and all the bad people who were out to get them. In reality he was the aggressor, the threat, but in the self-referential context of their private world, he was St. George, the dragon-slayer. It was a role he gloried in, for it gave him, simultaneously, sexual and emotional gratification, revenge against the Sharps for all their bad-mouthing of Doc Klenner over the years, plus a chance to play soldier. There must have been days when it was almost as good as being a real doctor.

The incidence of paranoid, persecutional behavior on the part of both people was constant and often extreme. There was Fritz writing life-threatening letters to himself; scratching himself with a knife and pretending the cuts were "wounds" he received in a scuffle with agents sent to assassinate his father; posing as a military superman, a super-warrior who jumped, 007-like, from assignment to assignment in dangerous climes, against enemies domestic and foreign; posing as a doctor; bragging about how he would be one of the leaders in whatever bizarre form of Fourth Reich emerged after Armageddon. And there was Susie, with her daily fear of kidnappers stalking the boys, her refusal to let them eat the cookies their grandmother baked for them because they might contain poison.

Ultimately, Susie had to choose between turning her back on all that she had been and known, or rejecting Fritz. She chose her cousin. Because Fritz had come to her when he did, because he had ingratiated himself so deeply in her feelings and beliefs, he had become closer to her than anyone else had been in her adult life. She joined him in the world of psychopathology he had created for her rather than lose that companionship.

It is always hard for people to comprehend how someone like Susie — well educated, well bred, surely well intentioned for most of her life — could fall into such a pit of delusion. Yet the power of shared psychosis is frequently underestimated.

One of the most compelling modern examples of the power of dual delusion is found in the final chapter of Robert Lindner's classic volume of psychoanalytic adventure stories, *The Fifty-Minute Hour* (new edition published in 1986 by Delta Books, a division of Dell Publishing Co.). Lindner was asked by a government agency to treat an otherwise brilliant physicist who had suddenly started falling behind in his work because, he claimed, he was spending too much of his time on another planet.

Once Lindner investigated the patient's delusion more deeply, he discovered that the man, called Kirk Allen in the book, had not only dreamed up a whole fantasy universe for himself, but had also meticulously documented it with a 12,000-page autobiography of himself as galactic emperor; 2,000 pages of historical, cultural, political, ecological, and genealogical data; 161 architectural sketches; astronomical charts; painstakingly scaled maps; and a whole series of carefully written scientific papers with titles such as "The Fauna of Srom Olma I," "History of the Intergalactic Scientific Institute," and "The Unique Brain Development of the Crystopeds of Srom Norba X."

So rich, elaborate, and deep-seated was Kirk Allen's delusion, so much more exciting and fulfilling than real life, that Lindner saw only one way to break through to his patient: to pretend to accept the delusion until its internal contradictions surfaced strongly enough to break down the facade. "In a sudden flash of inspiration," Lindner wrote, "it came to me that in order to separate Kirk from his madness, it was necessary for me to enter his fantasy and, from that position, try to pry him loose from the psychosis."

But, to his astonishment and dismay, Lindner found himself sucked into the fantasy, too. His description of the process could be applied, with only a few changes, to what happened to Fritz and Susie:

> We all of us possess areas of lessened resistance, and somewhere on the psychic armor of the strongest there is a vulnerable place. In this case it happened that the materials of Kirk's psychosis and the Achilles heel of my personality met and meshed like the gears of a clock.
>
> As the days passed…the symptoms…increased in number and intensity. They were all of an obsessional nature and, as such disturbances tend to do, they began to invade my thoughts and behavior to an even greater degree. Whereas the fantasy and its delights had previously beckoned only when I was with Kirk…it now intruded itself into moments when I was not fully engaged otherwise and even, on occasion, when I was attending to affairs far removed from Kirk and his delusion. I found myself, for example, translating certain words, terms and names into the 'Olmayan' language. Phrases in this weird tongue, unannounced and unbidden, often came into my thoughts and remained there to plague consciousness annoyingly like a haunting melody…At a startlingly rapid rate, it seems, larger and larger areas of my mind were being taken over by the fantasy.
>
> …Suffice it to say that, with the passage of time, all the manifestations of obsession I have mentioned intensified. The anxiety, for example, could no longer be passed off as inner excitement. To meet this rising tide, the obsessional demands increased and, in turn, the compulsive requirements from

thought and action became more exacting...other areas of my existence were invaded.

Eventually, Kirk Allen freed himself by simply growing tired of seeing his analyst being eaten alive by what had once been a snugly private fantasy. Lindner was delighted by the cure of his patient, but the experience shook him profoundly. His conclusion bears repeating for those who wonder how Susie could have fallen over the edge:

> Until Kirk Allen came into my life I had never doubted my own stability. The aberrations of my mind, so I had always thought, were for others. Tolerant, somewhat amused, indulgent, I held to the myth of my own mental impregnability. Superior in the knowledge that I, at least, was completely sane and could not — no matter what — be shaken from my sanity, I tended to regard the foibles of my fellows...with what I now know to have been contempt.
>
> I am shamed by this smugness. But now, as I listen from my chair behind the couch, I know better. I know that my chair and the couch are separated only by a thin line. I know that it is, after all, but a happier combination of accidents that determines, finally, who shall lie on that couch, and who shall sit behind it.

Notes Toward a Pathology of the Soul

I suspect that the first adult contact between Susie and Fritz was quite casual — a run-in at Doc Klenner's clinic, almost certainly. But it was enough to attract her to the Klenners' style of thinking, of making their own rules.

When Susie moved back from Albuquerque after her marriage failed, she heard things from her own family that she didn't especially like to hear: that she had a responsibility to make some sort of peace with Tom Lynch for the sake of her two sons, and that maybe she ought to take a hard look at herself, to see if some of her troubles were not at least partly attributable to her own attitudes. She refused to listen and became furiously angry at Mother for even bringing such things into the open. I think her hegira to Taiwan was motivated, in some way, by a desire to avoid confronting these problems head-on. But all she did was delay that confrontation, because the same topics came up as soon as she was back from the Orient. And her response, again, was to bristle at the very suggestion of critical introspection.

So relations between her and Mother were, sporadically at least, not terribly close. You could sense the beginnings of the alienation that was to destroy her affection for Mother later on. But Susie had to believe in somebody, and here was her cousin, Fritz Klenner, offering her a version of reality that was more congenial by far than the one other family members held out for her. Fritz's version didn't require her to consider that her own character might be flawed.

Susie saw her divorce from Tom Lynch not as a matter of mutual mistakes and changes, but as a personal affront. Tom had not followed the script. He had forced her to live in the wrong town, had messed up all her plans, and ruined her life.

And now, a few months after she got back from Taiwan and was forced to cope with all her problems again, here comes Fritz telling her that he had inside information which proved Tom Lynch was a mobster, a dope smuggler with KGB connections. Suddenly, for Susie, things grew clear again. Now she had a reason, other than her own frailties, to explain why things had gone wrong. She had already concluded that Tom was no good, and that was the reason her life had taken a wrong turn. Fritz's fantasies were a comforting confirmation.

That's a desolate place to be: always having to be right. If your view of things does not embrace forgiveness, and its corollary, redemption, then you have lots of reasons to be afraid. And somehow the message had gotten into Susie's head that doing wrong, being wrong, were not just unfortunate, but were unforgivable — and that they *ought* to be unforgivable.

Fritz offered her a way out of that spiral. He convinced her that everything "normal" was doomed anyway, that the coming apocalypse would wipe the slate clean for everybody. But if she joined forces with him, they could survive. Even better, when the smoke cleared after Armageddon, they would be free to live according to their own plans. In a weird way, he was almost offering her a promise of reincarnation. And she bought into it from the start. At that point in her life, it was just what she wanted to hear.

When Susie returned from New Mexico, full of wild tales about Tom Lynch's behavior, lovable ol' Doc Klenner listened to her and immediately diagnosed Tom's problem as "drugs." All Fritz had to do was hear "drugs" from his Daddy, and it would have been just a short leap for him to come up with the notion that Tom Lynch was dealing in them as well as taking them. Fritz's fantasy creations had just enough connective tissue with possible realities to make it hard for people to call him a lunatic when he started spouting this stuff. Tom Lynch would not be the first dentist in recorded history to have started munching the fiorinol.

So Fritz first wove this web of half-plausible, extrapolated stuff, very tenuous at first, then gradually turned it into a web of iron. He didn't say things that were obviously deluded. He didn't come up to Susie and tell her that Albuquerque had been invaded by the body snatchers and Tom had been turned into a pod-person. She never would have joined with that kind of fantasy. But like Susie's own exaggerated tales about Tom, Fritz made sure his fables contained enough elements of half-truth, of extrapolated plausibility, for her to buy them.

I don't think Fritz made up this stuff for the sole purpose of suborning my sister's common sense. I think he actually believed these fables. It was his aura of genuine conviction, together with the element of plausibility, that got my sister hooked. If it had been a different, less subtle kind of craziness, she would have balked from the start.

Whether she bought all of the survivalist party-line is also debatable. It would depend on the circumstances. It might look plausible on Tuesday and flaky on Thursday. The reason I think she didn't accept it completely is that she still had all these plans for her future, dreams that were always coming up in conversations with friends and family. People who really expect Armageddon to descend in the next year or two don't go out and enroll in business school.

Susie's belief that her husband Tom had failed her and two-timed her was the opening wedge that set her up for the arrival of Fritz Klenner. Fritz psyched her out quickly, played his subtle domination games with her, and some kind of extreme chemical reaction took place between the two of them. What began as just one more seduction and domination game for Fritz quickly escalated out of control. Suddenly there were the makings of a serious, shared, delusional psychosis.

My sister's sense of security and self-esteem had been defined, until now, by a very particular set of circumstances. A certain kind

149

of family background, a certain kind of marriage, certain types of kids, a life that goes certain places in certain ways. One had just the right sort of bank balance, lived in just the right section of town, had a certain amount of income, and so on. These were the things that enabled my sister to feel safe, and that she was worth something. And then everything just crumbled.

CHAPTER THIRTY-THREE

Closing In

On Tuesday, May 21, 1985, after he had returned from making the funeral arrangements for his parents and grandmother, Robert Newsom III had a memorable conversation with detective Allen Gentry. The detective was still trying to fathom who could have possibly killed three innocent people like Robert Jr., Florence, and Hattie Newsom. Routinely, Gentry asked if there were anyone in the family who had an unusual interest in firearms.

You bet there is, replied Bob III: "My cousin, Fritz Klenner."

Bob III had suspected that Fritz was involved since the very night, two days before, when the horrific murders had been discovered. While a friend was driving him back home to Greensboro from the crime scene near Winston-Salem, they actually passed by the back entrance to the Friendly Hills apartment complex where Fritz and Susie lived. The sensation of being this close to the probable killer filled Newsom with a dark, atavistic urge. At the last minute, however, he decided not to turn in to see if Fritz's Blazer was there. He was unarmed, emotionally overwrought, and not sure he could control himself in a face-to-face encounter.

Fritz was there when Gentry and SBI detective Tom Sturgill finally got their chance to interview Susie on Wednesday, May 22. The apartment was a mess, overflowing with so much camping gear and clutter that whole piles of stuff had to be shifted just to provide the two officers with places to sit.

The officers noticed two things right away: Susie did not act like someone who has just lost her parents and grandmother to a violent crime, and Fritz was wearing a survival knife.

But Susie was talkative. She babbled on about what a nice woman her grandmother had been and complained about what a mess the cops had made of the Valley Road house during their crime-scene activities. She volunteered nothing about the upcoming custody battle against Tom Lynch for their boys, however. The omission struck Gentry as odd, because he had learned enough about the situation to know that it had to be, after the deaths of her family, the most important topic on her mind.

Where was she on Saturday, the day the murders took place? Oh, she spent the entire day with her old friend, Annette Hunt, and then she took her boys John and Jim out for supper, and then they all came back here to the apartment. And Fritz? He had been off camping in the Virginia mountains, one of his favorite pastimes. She and the boys had driven up to join him on Sunday afternoon, and when they got back one of the chows had run off and Fritz spent four hours tracking him down.

A family friend called sometime around midnight on Sunday, she said, and told her there had been "an accident" at Hattie Newsom's house in Old Town. But the murders had not been confirmed until about two a.m.

How had Susie reacted when the news came? She had stayed up all night, working on a term paper. As for Fritz, he had just curled up on the floor, the way he often did, and gone to sleep.

When Gentry and Sturgill started quizzing Susie about the killings of Delores and Jane Lynch ten months before, they got a surprising earful. Her mother- and sister-in-law had been snuffed in a professional hit, Susie told them — even though Kentucky police were still labeling it a "foiled robbery."

Now Susie began to talk about her custody fight with her ex-husband. Tom Lynch had inherited a lot of money after his mother was murdered, and he was deploying that money now on the legal battlefield. Tom was a mobster, too — didn't Gentry know? — and he had connections with some of the biggest dope dealers in the Southwest. Big-league mafia. While she talked, Susie occasionally reached out and patted Fritz, as though reaffirming the circuit between them.

Fritz would protect them, Susie insisted, winding up her testimony. As Gentry rose to leave, he turned his attention, without preamble, to Fritz. What line of work was Fritz in?

"I'm a doctor," Fritz assured them, unruffled. But not, alas, licensed to practice in this state. Not yet, anyhow.

On Friday, Gentry had a long chat with Annie Hill Klenner, Fritz's mother. Oh yes, Annie Hill knew that Fritz lived at Susie's apartment. But unlike some people, she didn't have a filthy mind about the relationship. Fritz was just there to help his cousin through some rough times, that was all. He was training the chows to be guard dogs. Susie had been attacked one night, on her way back from taking out the garbage. Didn't the police know that? The dogs had saved her.

No, Annie Hill admitted, Susie had not been getting along too well with her late mother recently. She had turned to the Klenner side of the family instead, and now she had long, warm talks with Annie Hill just like she used to have with Florence in her younger days.

Fritz's new line of work, his secret work for the government, had really made a man out of him, his mother thought. But it was sometimes dangerous, not just for Fritz but for all of them. There had even been a bomb delivered to her house, she said, intended for Fritz. Luckily, he had warned her about the package in time and had used his special training to defuse it. And just recently, some SBI agents had searched Fritz's Blazer and done extensive damage to it.

At this point, Gentry looked sideways at his partner for the day, J.W. Bryant, who *was* an SBI agent. Bryant's expression clearly indicated that this was big news to him.

Gentry next asked what Fritz had been doing on Saturday. Oh, said Annie Hill, he had gone camping up in the Virginia mountains with an old friend of his named Ian Perkins.

The following Tuesday, May 28, Gentry and Sturgill made an unannounced visit to Susie's apartment. They needed to speak to Fritz, they said. Susie fetched him. He ambled out of the back bedroom, wearing a one-piece war surplus flight suit. Would he mind joining them down at the SBI office for an interview? Sure thing, just let him get dressed.

When he returned, he was still attired in paramilitary style, this time wearing khaki pants and a survival knife on his belt. Gentry and Sturgill drove Fritz to the SBI office for questioning.

Alone with Fritz now, and operating from a growing certainty that they had a first-rate suspect as well as a certified weirdo on their hands, the two cops grilled Fritz pretty hard. When they poked him about his status as a doctor, he bridled angrily: "I don't see that topic as relevant!"

As for his whereabouts on the weekend of the murders, he had picked up his friend, Ian Perkins, at Perkins's rooming house near the Washington and Lee campus in Lexington, Virginia, at midnight on Friday. Then they drove up to the campgrounds at Peaks of Otter, Virginia. They registered there at campsite such-and-such and he had a receipt to prove it. With a flourish, he produced the little document from his billfold.

He and Perkins slept late on Saturday, took a night hike that evening, and broke camp at noon on Sunday. At Perkins's rooming house, Fritz showered, called Susie, and arranged to meet her at Natural Bridge — a popular tourist spot in the Virginia mountains — for dinner with the boys. Afterward, he took the boys for a hike. Then they all drove to Greensboro, where he spent the remainder of Sunday night searching for Susie's wayward chow dog.

Fritz tried to take the offensive in the interrogation: Didn't they understand that Susie was in danger? He had installed a dead-bolt lock on her door to protect her when he wasn't around. To substantiate this, Fritz held up and wiggled a key ring at the two detectives. Both of them instantly recognized the familiar and unique shape of another key on the ring — a handcuff key. What in the world was Fritz doing with a handcuff key? Nothing in their observations of either the couple or their living quarters led them to suspect kinky sexual practices. The decor of the Friendly Hills apartment was simply not consistent with swingers and bondage games.

The way Fritz handled this grilling was straight out of the survival textbooks and training manuals. He was cool, quick, consistent with his alibi, and just a little bit aggressive. It was, both lawmen agreed, an impressive performance. But they definitely thought it was a performance. They agreed they had a very promising suspect. The way to nail him might be through his camping buddy, Ian Perkins.

And so, on May 30, Gentry and Sturgill drove up to Washington and Lee University to have a little talk with Ian. They had already put some heat on Ian by visiting his mother earlier that week, asking a few questions. They knew she would give her son the disconcerting news that he was a major figure in the alibi of a murder suspect. Ian's mother did tell him, and Ian had been stewing for several days, exactly as Gentry and Sturgill had planned.

Indeed, by the time they got to Ian, he was not calm. At first, Ian told them a story that more or less dovetailed with Fritz's. But unlike Fritz, Ian was quite visibly nervous. Fritz had warned him that it might be necessary to lie, but assured him it was all in the interests of national security. His future employers at the Agency would be watching to see how he performed under pressure.

Ian wasn't performing worth a damn, and he knew it. He was sweating, chain-smoking, dry-mouthed, and his hands trembled. After fifteen minutes of moderate grilling by the two experienced officers, Ian Perkins could see his future CIA career going belly-up.

When Ian had finished stumbling through his cover story, Gentry began, in a not unkindly fashion, to review the discrepancies and inconsistencies. There were several facts that didn't add up, and Ian was not ready to handle it. He started stumbling badly, backtracking, making new mistakes. The bottom line, Gentry informed him, was that Ian now looked very much like a prime accessory to three brutal murders. They were talking hard time now — measured in years, not months.

Ian cracked. In moments he was sobbing out his story. Yes, they had been in Winston-Salem Saturday night, not at the campground in Virginia; and yes, Fritz had told him about killing some people. But it had been a CIA mission, and that made it all right.

At last, the young college student realized that he'd been duped. Knowing that his cooperation would be weighed against his culpability for what he now understood to have been a violent murder spree,

Ian Perkins turned state's evidence.

CHAPTER THIRTY-FOUR

'I Won't See You Again.'

The police wanted to prepare the strongest possible case against Fritz Klenner, so they asked Ian Perkins if he was willing to be wired for sound in an attempt to draw Fritz into an admission of guilt. Ian, anxious to make up for his unwitting role in the Newsom murders, agreed to go along.

So on June 1, 1985, a thin, flat recorder was taped to Ian Perkins's back, and his belt was bugged with a tiny transmitter. Ian had some trouble staying calm. It was not unreasonable to think that Fritz would kill him if he discovered the ruse.

The meeting began in the parking lot of a shopping mall in Reidsville. They were under surveillance by five carloads of SBI agents and Forsyth County detectives stationed at various points in the vicinity. Ian walked over to Fritz's Blazer and climbed in — blithely unaware, as was everyone, of the bomb Fritz had bolted under the seats of his Blazer months before.

"Let's ride somewhere," Fritz suggested.

Fritz and Ian drove slowly past modest frame houses, little brick office buildings, curb markets, and fast-food emporiums...small-town North Carolina in the early summer light, when the greens are still fresh and before the lawns acquire that baked and dusty look of late summer. School would be letting out that week. The lawns looked as if they were waiting for children. It all seemed an incongruous background for a discussion of murders and secret missions. And yet what had drawn Fritz and Ian together in the first place was their shared and passionate conviction that all of this, as mundane and even as tacky as some of it might be, was worth dying for, or killing for.

While they were driving around, Ian told Fritz how detective Gentry and the SBI agents had grilled him. "They told me the murders had taken place on Saturday night. I was sweating. I hope I didn't seem too nervous. I was scared to death."

Fritz then gave Perkins a capsule, telling him that the drug, papaverine, would calm him down. Ian swallowed the pill without question. The eavesdropping officers blanched: The kid hadn't been in the car with Fritz for five minutes before he was swallowing a Young Doctor Klenner pill. It could be anything, including poison.

Fritz tried to reassure Ian. One of those SBI agents, he ventured, might have been a CIA observer, "a Company person who was there to test your reactions."

Perkins let that one slide by. He then went over in some detail the whole Peaks of Otter cover story, trying to tell Fritz exactly what he had told the lawmen. Fritz suggested they drive back up to Virginia in the morning and create the remains of a campfire alongside the trail they had supposedly hiked on the night of the murders. Perkins said he couldn't: "I got this polygraph thing."

"Oh, it's tomorrow morning?" said Fritz. "Okay, you do not have to take the polygraph." Fritz assured him that refusing to do so was within his legal rights.

Ian objected. "Be kind of suspicious if I backed out of it. I'm going through with it. I've just really got to get myself composed."

"That's a tactic people like that use," replied Fritz. "If they really were going to give you a hard time, they would want you to do the polygraph then, not give you three or four days to think about it. See, that's psychological. They want to get your head screwed out. You always have the option to tell them that."

"You don't see any need for it?" Ian asked. Fritz grew thoughtful. At the other end of the transmitter, Gentry could almost hear the gears turning in Fritz's mind.

Finally Fritz had an answer. "All you have to say is that…mmmm…you're privy to information that falls under the National Security Act."

Ian was doubtful. "What if they ask about that?"

"Say nothing," said Fritz.

"The name-rank-and-serial-number deal?" said Perkins. "I think I can remember that. I'm sorry. This has been eating me up. I didn't sleep at all last night."

Fritz again admonished Perkins to stone-wall, citing one of their mutual heroes: "…like Gordon Liddy and the Watergate thing." Never even tell them you belong to an organization, Fritz went on. "Just say that you have been advised that taking a polygraph, that — just say flat that you are not to take one under any circumstances because of information that could be divulged indirectly in questioning. See, this is all mind games. They like to play with your head."

"Yeah," Ian replied.

"I'll give you a phenobarb tablet to take so you can get a good night's sleep tonight," said Fritz.

"I feel better just talking to you."

"Okay," Fritz continued, "now what you've got to do in the next forty-eight hours, you have to develop a mind-set. You have to tell yourself you were in Peaks of Otter."

"It has to be the truth?" Ian asked.

"That's right. You were not in Winston-Salem, so you can't say that you were in Winston-Salem."

Now Fritz's voice grew thick with emotion as he fumbled for something in the Blazer. For a moment, he seemed close to tears. "I'll lend you something that Dad gave me the first time I ever went on any type of covert operation. These are scapulars that come from, well, it would be in East Germany, today. This one was his mother's sacred heart, and this one was his father's. They got those as children at the Shrine of Mary of the Hills, on a pilgrimage, the night before my family came to this country. I've always found great comfort in these."

The conversation then switched to the subject of prescription drugs and which sort of "downers" might best prepare a man for a polygraph test. Fritz offered Perkins some Valium.

The conversation began to wind down. Finally, Ian said: "I better be getting on back…I don't think I'll ever be as scared as I was yesterday."

Again, Fritz tried soothe Perkins. "Did you ever think, Ian, you don't have to prove anything? What they're doing — they have nothing…they're fishing."

"When they told me it was late Saturday night that this happened," Ian said, referring to the Newsom killings, "it took sheer force of will to keep from falling apart right there."

"I still haven't heard any actual confirmation of when it occurred," mused Fritz. He'd been following all the newspaper accounts, and the estimates given in those stories had ranged from Friday night to Sunday morning.

Ian was not so easily reassured: "What really scared me was when they said a .45 was used."

"They haven't given a caliber that's been released in the paper that I'm aware of," said Fritz. "There was an article yesterday in which they were saying it was not the same type gun as what was used out in Kentucky. What I suspect is that it probably was a fairly professional thing, that Tom had his sister and mother killed, and I would not be surprised if he were not behind this. Even if it was a .45, Ian, for a professional, that's not much of a coincidence at all. I mean .45 and .22 are the most commonly used weapons because they are subsonic."

By now they had arrived back in the mall parking lot. As they parted, Fritz said, "I want to see you sometime tomorrow before you take off, because I want to see how this medicine's working."

"Well," said Perkins, opening the door and getting out, "I'll be talking to you."

Indeed he would, the very next day, Sunday, June 2. This time, Gentry and Sturgill rehearsed Perkins, telling him how to ask the kind of leading questions that were needed to draw Fritz into some really incriminating admissions.

The second taped meeting between Ian and Fritz also took place in a mall parking lot, this time in Greensboro. During their phone conversation earlier that morning to set up the rendezvous, Ian had told Fritz that Gentry and Sturgill had picked him up the previous night at his mother's house and had taken him to the scene of the Newsom killings on Valley Road in Old Town. It was the first thing Ian brought up when he met with Fritz at the Greensboro mall.

"Really scared the shit out of me!" Perkins breathed, as he slid through the Blazer's passenger door — still unaware of the bomb bolted beneath the seat. "I saw the gold car and went into the house. It was a mess. It was right down the road from where I dropped you off. I believe we were on a government mission, but I think there's something that just ain't kosher here. I'd like to know what's going on..."

"Gold car?" muttered Fritz, suddenly concerned that something indeed might not be kosher. "What gold car did they show you?"

"The one you had."

"The car I had was brown," Fritz quickly insisted.

"I thought it was gold," pressed Ian.

"The car I had was brown," Fritz growled, as if saying it would make it so, and convince Perkins it was so.

"They showed me a car," Perkins continued, following his rehearsed script rather bravely. "It was right down the road from where I let you off. That scared me...I didn't know what to think. I don't think you're lying to me or withholding anything..."

Fritz must have sensed now the full extent of his folly in taking Perkins along on his mission. It was damage-control time.

"Ian," he began, taking a new tack — suavely, wearily, a man misunderstood and unjustly doubted. "Ian, I have never been to Nana's house. I do not know where it is. It could have been in the same area. I couldn't take you there if my life depended on it."

Fritz made a dramatic flourish and deposited in Ian's sweating hands a file folder containing a small sheaf of papers and a few photographs of tough, vaguely Third World-looking individuals. The papers were full of bureaucratic mumbo-jumbo and virtually every name, date, or fact that could specify their origin or actual meaning had been blacked out. It was the *Time* magazine photo ploy all over again, probably something Fritz had whipped up the night before

161

when he realized Perkins was wavering.

"I want you to look at that…I wish they had not had some stuff deleted, but you understand. At this point, you just do not need to know." Fritz tapped the photographs. "These are the people who were in the house. They're the ones who went down the other night. That's the one I had to hit five times."

"God," muttered Perkins. "The one with the hat is one of the big — "

"One of the big guys? Yeah . . . he was on the patio."

"Which one did you use the knife on?" asked Ian.

"I used the knife on this guy, and I used the knife on, on this one, because he was still showing signs."

After getting Perkins to describe where Nana Newsom's house really was, Fritz drew a sketchy diagram showing how he had actually gone off to a side street. The proximity of the hit and of the Newsom residence was just a ghastly coincidence.

Perkins confessed he was so nervous about the whole business that he'd thrown up. Fritz handed him some Valium and asked if Perkins were still slated for a polygraph test. Ian affirmed that he was.

"See, what they are figuring, that they can play mind games with you. They found very little physical evidence. In fact, nothing to connect anything to anything. See, they figured you're the youngest. Actually, it should make you mad. They figured if I was a pro, if I'd done something, they weren't going to get ape-shit with me. They figured you're the youngest, that you were the weak link…"

"I want to do the right thing," Ian assured Fritz. "I won't crack. I don't know if they'll leave me alone after this, but I don't think I'll have any problems. You know, they tried to tell me you weren't a doctor. Course, I didn't believe that. I know you've been in medical school. I know you were doing your residency when Doctor [Klenner] died…"

"Ian, the reason I have not started practice — I went to Duke — I told you, I've been doing stuff. I first got contacted when I was at Woodward [Academy], and off and on over the years, when they check anything, when I went to Duke I was enrolled there, which is in the process of being straightened out now. When Dad died was an

162

inopportune time."

"They gave you your provisional license?" asked Ian.

"Oh, yeah. When I was traveling, see, I went to several meetings and places you don't need to know about right now."

"I don't think I want to," agreed Ian.

"But when I was in school, it was better for all concerned that I wasn't traceable back to Reidsville." Fritz firmly removed the file from Perkins's lap. "I wanted you to see this, so you'd have something to sink your teeth into. I know you trust me."

In parting, Fritz gave Perkins a spray can of aluminum chlorhydrate — prescription-strength antiperspirant. "Any time you have to talk with anybody, spray the palms of your hands, your feet, real good. Saturate a cotton ball, wipe your face. That'll keep you from perspiring."

"If I get any anxiety attacks...I'll call you for sure," Perkins said as he climbed out of Fritz's Blazer, heaving a vast internal sigh of relief.

As damning as the first two tapes were, the law officers who reviewed them wanted Perkins to get yet another tape, to really nail the case shut. Ian consented. He met with Fritz again on Monday, June 3. The complete transcript of the third tape has never been released. But from excerpts made public, it seems as though, at the beginning of the conversation, Fritz was still cool, still a touch arrogant, still convinced he could bob and weave his way out of the Newsom murders with a tap-dance and a few more lies. He never came right out and admitted killing the Newsoms, but he made enough admissions tying him to the murder scene on that specific night to justify the issuance of a warrant for his arrest.

But then Fritz realized, midway into the third and final conversation with Ian, that the reckoning was closer at hand than he had imagined, and he got spooked. After absolving Ian of responsibility for any wrongdoing, Fritz broke off their final dialogue with a curt, tense farewell: "I've got things to do...I won't see you again."

An Ironclad Case

Why didn't the law move in and pick up Fritz when he was alone and vulnerable? Why did they wait so long to go after him? And then, when they did make their move, why did they make such a botch of it?

Those are big questions, because if they had taken Fritz after hearing the first or second taped conversation with Ian Perkins, at least three more people probably would be alive today.

Let's go back and start answering those questions by taking as cool and objective a look as possible at Fritz's actions on the night he murdered Bob, Florence, and Hattie Newsom.

Much of what he did that night *was* top-notch professional work. But some of what he did was addled, stupid, and amateurish. The mixture of sober professionalism and giddy improvisation was a function of his inability to distinguish between objective reality and his own fantasies.

I think he was probably going along fine and calm and keeping to the program until he couldn't find one of his empty shell casings. That must have driven him stark raving nuts.

His plan seems to have been to steal Nana's gold Plymouth, drive it to Charlotte, then ditch it to help create the impression of a robbery and a getaway. That's probably why he told Ian about a mythical mission in Charlotte. But then he gets out on the road and finds out, first, that the car he's chosen is not going to make it to Charlotte, and second, that the Winston-Salem police are pretty diligent when it comes to checking out suspicious automobiles in the middle of the night. So he had Ian follow him back to the Newsom house, and he returned the car and made these addle-brained attempts to cover his tracks by breaking a window in the back door. But he got rattled again, and for some peculiar reason he leaves the keys sticking in the door beneath the broken glass.

Then he goes back into the house and tries to cover his tracks by starting a fire. But what does he do? He doesn't go to the car and siphon out a pint of gasoline and douse it over the wooden furniture or something else equally flammable. No, he just throws a bunch of papers in the middle of a rug and starts a tiny fire that is virtually guaranteed to extinguish itself within minutes.

There's no logic at work any more. There's just the aimless knee-jerk actions of a man who thinks he can get away with murder simply because of who and what he thinks he is.

And then there's the dumbest mistake of all — taking Ian Perkins along in the first place. Fritz didn't need Ian for anything, really. Fritz had his own car and plenty of firepower for the job, and he must have known that if anything did go wrong, Perkins, not himself, was the one most likely to attract attention or spill his guts if someone stopped them. The only conceivable reason he brought Perkins along was just so he could show off, to prove to somebody besides Susie what a big secret agent he was. Perkins was so worshipful, so blissfully naive. My guess is that Fritz just couldn't resist playing to that kind of an audience.

But then, once Fritz gets out on the highway and inhales a few gulps of fresh air, he becomes himself again, calms down, and by the time he gets stopped by the Winston-Salem patrolman, he is once again the coolest customer you'd ever meet. That patrolman, by the way, is one lucky man. If he had stopped Fritz a few miles closer to the house, while he was still rattled, Fritz would have almost certainly come out of the car shooting.

Okay, so what kind of case do we have, even without a single tape?

First, we have Ian Perkins's testimony about the elaborate construction of an alibi — the camping trip to Peaks of Otter, Virginia — and how they actually snuck out of the camp and drove to Winston-Salem on Saturday night. That is a damning piece of evidence right there, and the sort of thing a prosecuting attorney could really sink his teeth into.

Second, we have Ian's testimony that he let Fritz out at the bottom of the hill leading to Hattie Newsom's house on Valley Road, on the same night they were murdered.

Third, we have Ian's testimony that Fritz showed up an hour or so later driving a car whose description matched that of Hattie Newsom's car.

Fourth, we have Ian's testimony that Fritz was stopped, shortly thereafter, by an officer of the Winston-Salem Police Department. This is evidence that can be corroborated by checking the tapes of police transmissions for that night. They would prove that Fritz was stopped exactly where and when Ian said he was stopped. The license plate number is recorded on the tape, identifying the vehicle's legal owner. So this car not only looks like Hattie Newsom's car, it *is* her car. We have Fritz riding around in my grandmother's auto a mere ninety minutes or so after she was killed.

Fifth, we have Ian's testimony that he saw Fritz destroy his outer garments, which surely had traces of blood and gunpowder on them. We also have Ian's testimony that Fritz later buried a knife and threw away the barrel from his National Match Colt .45.

Sixth, we have Fritz going home and jewelling the extractor of that pistol, just after the murders, even though the manufacturer's records of that weapon would indicate it was sold without such a modification.

And finally, we have the police, back at the Valley Road house, finding a recently fired .45-caliber shell casing lodged on top of a piece of furniture in the hallway where my father died.

Conclusion: A really aggressive prosecutor could have nailed Fritz without any tapes at all. Thousands of men have gone to the gallows on far less evidence than what the police had before they wired Perkins for sound. I'm a lawyer myself, and I'm certain I could have tried him without the tapes before one hundred juries and won a conviction from ninety of them.

With the first and second tapes, even an inept prosecutor would have had Fritz dead-to-rights. Just look at what he admits to on that second tape. He admits to killing people in Winston-Salem on that weekend, and he admits to using a knife on one of them. Good Lord, I could try him before a thousand juries with that kind of evidence and get a conviction from every one of them, no problem at all! We have him creating an alibi, we have him in the victim's car on the night of the crime, we have him destroying evidence, and we have physical evidence at the scene of the crime which is consistent with the informer's testimony.

With that second tape, he's just down the tubes. He's cooked.

So why didn't the police take him after they heard that second tape? They had plenty of time to arrest him safely.

Alternatively, they could have taken him while he was driving back to Susie's apartment after the third tape. But that last remark of Fritz's — "I've got things to do...I won't see you again" — must have sounded to the police like he was getting ready to flee their jurisdiction. They got tangled up in their own feet at that point.

The key question, the one on which several lives pivoted, was why the law even wanted that third tape. It has never been released, but according to people who have heard it, who gave depositions during our private investigation, it was a disappointment. It wasn't really worth the trouble of setting up, in terms of admissible evidence.

I do not blame the Greensboro Police Department. Most of those guys didn't even know what was going down until just a few minutes before the action started. I don't really blame any of the officers involved.

It was a headless operation, though, and it lacked the two elements that a complicated bust must have: command and control.

I shall state it plainly, for it's a classic example of why police officers in the field hate it when a district attorney tries to run a case like this: The Forsyth County D.A. apparently wanted an airtight case before hauling Fritz in. The murder victims were prominent, popular people; the suspect was a member of a prominent, popular family; and the woman with him was the niece of a state supreme court justice. He wanted a sure thing. He wanted nothing less than a flat-out, cut-and-dried confession on tape from Fritz Klenner: "Yes, I came to Winston-Salem and murdered the Newsom family!" But

Fritz, no matter *how* rattled he may have become, was never crazy enough to say something like that.

CHAPTER THIRTY-SIX

A Cluster of Cops

It was on Monday, June 3, 1985, in front of the Zayre discount store at the O. Henry Shopping Center on Cone Boulevard in Greensboro, that Fritz Klenner and Ian Perkins had their third and final meeting. Again, it had taken place in Fritz's Blazer. It lasted less than fifteen minutes. And from the point of view of the numerous law enforcement personnel listening in via Ian's hidden microphone, it was a disappointment. Fritz added nothing new to the admissions he had already made on the first two tapes.

After Fritz uttered his final statement to Perkins — "I've got things to do...I won't see you again" — Ian bade farewell and walked away from the Blazer, his shoulders trembling with relief. Ian would have been even more relieved had he realized that during all three meetings in Fritz's Blazer, he had been sitting on top of a powerful bomb.

The police, however, were not at all relieved. Fritz's final remarks galvanized them. At one point in the transmitted conversation, when Fritz realized a warrant for his arrest would surely be issued within a matter of hours, he spoke darkly about "popping a capsule." Nobody wanted Fritz to kill himself before he answered some hard questions, so the operation suddenly acquired a helter-skelter urgency.

Suicide wasn't the only possibility, either. It also seemed plausible that Fritz could throw a few guns into the Blazer and make a run for it out of local jurisdiction. This would make it much harder to apprehend him. He might even head out to New Mexico to hit Tom

Lynch. It was urgent to stop him as soon as possible.

A sizable law enforcement task force followed Fritz back to Susie's Friendly Hills apartment. This took twenty minutes or so because of Fritz's habitual slow driving. In one car was SBI agent Sturgill, detective Gentry, and another Forsyth County sheriff's detective named John Boner. A third car was driven by Greensboro Police Department detective A.G. Travis, who had been appointed liaison officer for the operation only that morning and was unaware of exactly what he was getting into. Also in the car with Travis was SBI agent Ed Hunt, supervisor of the regional SBI administrative district; Captain Ron Barker of the Forsyth County Sheriff's Department; and Lieutenant Dan Davidson of the Oldham County Police Department in Kentucky, who had just arrived in Greensboro and was anxious to be in on the resolution of a case which had bedeviled him for month after frustrating month. Also trailing Fritz, in a blue Mustang, were Oldham County detectives Lynn Nobles and Sherman Childers — two of the original investigators of the Lynch killings. Driving the Mustang was Terry Spainhour, a Forsyth County deputy sheriff.

Astonishingly, none of these law enforcement officers was carrying a valid arrest warrant. To take care of that oversight, Sturgill pulled over and made an urgent call to Forsyth County District Attorney Don Tisdale. Sturgill recounted Fritz's final ominous remarks and at last received authorization to make an arrest.

Sturgill, Gentry, and Boner then hurried back to the local SBI office to exchange their car for an SBI vehicle in order to have better radio communications. It didn't do them much good. The frequencies used by the several law enforcement agencies involved in the operation were incompatible. Later, when Guilford County deputies and additional Greensboro police officers got involved, they were unable to communicate directly with their opposite numbers from the SBI and Forsyth County Sheriff's Department. Some cars which could see each other could not talk to each other. The central clearing point for much of the radio traffic was the dispatcher's office at the Greensboro Police Department, but nobody on duty there had the foggiest idea what was going on, who was being pursued, what kind of vehicle the suspect was driving, or whether or not the suspect was heavily armed.

When Fritz arrived back at Susie's apartment, just after two p.m., the place was ringed with five cars full of armed lawmen. None of the vehicles, however, were marked cars. In position around the apartment, and in a nearby supermarket parking lot, were: a burgundy Chevy Impala (SBI agent J.W. Bryant and deputy sheriff Stephen Carden) parked to cover the rear entrance to the apartment; a tan Buick Riviera (Travis, Hunt, Barker, and Davidson); a gray, motorpool-looking Ford Victoria (Gentry, Sturgill, and Boner); a blue Mustang (Nobles, Childers, and Spainhour); and a wine-colored Camaro (Forsyth County deputy Marc Fetter and SBI agent Walt House). None of these men was wearing a uniform.

In addition to the officers' personal sidearms, each car also carried at least one high-powered rifle and shotgun. Overhead, an SBI spotter plane flew surveillance patterns over the Friendly Hills apartment complex.

Nobody wanted to go in after Fritz. Susie's apartment, they knew, contained a small arsenal and vast quantities of ammunition. Gentry and Sturgill, who had become familiar with the place during their visits to question Susie, were fairly certain there would be explosives, too. Given even a few seconds' warning, Fritz could mount an all-day standoff from inside the apartment, and it was a good bet he wouldn't stop shooting until he was killed or until he decided to kill himself. Because Susie Newsom was also in the apartment, which was located in a busy residential area, the prospects for digging Fritz out of the apartment were not good. He could turn the place into Iwo Jima if he saw them coming.

They decided to try to lure him out. Sturgill phoned the apartment. Susie answered. Could Fritz please meet them down at the SBI office? He's not home, Susie lied. Try again about seven.

What kind of dialogue was going on inside the apartment between Fritz and Susie is anybody's guess. It is possible that they had rehearsed some sort of emergency getaway drill many times before. After all, Fritz had been foretelling a day of reckoning, whether it was from Russian missiles, hordes of rampaging mongrel minorities, or Tom Lynch's mafia buddies. Well, here it was. Condition Red, everybody! Execute Plan Omega!

While Fritz and Susie packed, Fritz found time for some final communications with the outside world. He scrawled several notes on sheets of stationery still bearing the imprint of Dr. Frederick C. Klenner, M.D. In his first note, he wrote:

"This is to certify that my friend Ian Perkins was in no way involved in any wrongdoings of any kind. He was with me on a camping trip to the Peaks of Otter on the weekend of May 18th and to the best of his certain knowledge in training for a possible career in covert operations."

In a second note, Fritz seemed to anticipate being gone for a long time. He took curious pains to establish the ownership of much of the stuff he was about to leave behind:

"The firearms in this apartment and in the Blazer were the property of Fred R. Klenner, Sr., and are the property of Annie Sharp Klenner, as are the computer, TV, electronics equipment, weight machines, and camping gear."

In a third note, Fritz made a strange attempt to deny guilt, to shift blame to outside forces, and to justify his own existence — all in three sentences:

"I have in my life never physically harmed anyone as in taking human life. I am innocent of any accusations that have come to my attention and fear an elaborate frame. I have spent my life in the service of God, my country and my family."

And finally, there was one brief personal message that sounds very much like a man saying his last goodbye:

"Mother, I love you now and always."

The three more formal notes were signed "Fred R. Klenner Jr." The note to his mother was simply signed, "Your Fritz."

Meanwhile, in the stakeout around the apartment, the police were figuring that, wherever Fritz was going to be at seven o'clock, it was a good bet he had no intention of being in that apartment. Gentry and Sturgill decided they had to go in and try to make the arrest right away. They also decided it would be more effective psychologically if they went in with a uniformed police officer, for appearance's sake. A call went in for assistance. Tommy Dennis, a veteran Greensboro police officer, drew the assignment. He was on patrol near the Greensboro Coliseum at the time.

While Dennis was driving to the Friendly Hills apartment complex, Fritz came out and started loading equipment into his Blazer. Susie came out, too, and began piling duffel bags into the hulking black vehicle. Then Fritz put what appeared to be several automatic weapons into the Blazer. The watching officers felt mounting alarm.

Their concern increased when Susie's two sons suddenly appeared. John and Jim were supposed to be in school — but here they were, dutifully climbing into the Blazer, dressed in camouflage outfits like little versions of Fritz. Now the situation was much more complicated.

Susie's chow dogs also hopped into the Blazer. When everybody was tucked in, Fritz backed the vehicle out of his parking slot and drove slowly toward the main gate, where the apartment complex driveways join Friendly Avenue.

Law enforcement vehicles converged on the spot in a wild scramble. At that moment, Officer Dennis arrived, driving an unmarked black Malibu with a blue light on top. He pulled up alongside the Ford and the Mustang on Friendly Avenue. Gentry leaned out and quickly tried to tell Dennis what was happening: murder suspect, big black Blazer, be here any second now. If you've got an armored vest, better strap it on fast. Dennis was already wearing his vest that day. His wife had insisted.

After Fritz turned out onto Friendly Avenue, the melee that followed made the intersection, for a few moments, look like the bumper-car ride at a county fair. Cop cars slid in at different angles. Travis maneuvered the Buick in front of the Blazer, while other officers held their badges out of windows and shook them at Fritz. Fritz looked amazed. It was really happening at last! Yet no one saw even a trace of fear on his face. Calmly, Fritz swerved the Blazer onto the curb.

Travis's Buick, positioned in front of the Blazer, picked that critical moment to stall. Fritz zig-zagged around the inert Buick and started driving, at a maddeningly slow pace, down Friendly Avenue toward central Greensboro. Tommy Dennis saw the big black four-by-four coming straight for him. He switched on his flashing blue light and made a U-turn to bring himself close behind the Blazer. This was a textbook felony-stop. But at this point, a civilian car, traveling in the same direction as Fritz, began to slow down. Its driver, seeing the flashing blue lights, assumed it was she who was being signaled to stop.

Just as things were getting dangerously congested, the Camaro driven by Officer Fetter came barreling out of the Friendly Hills entrance and tried to slice in front of Fritz. Dennis had to take evasive action to avoid being struck by the Camaro. Still handling himself like a pro, Fritz again outflanked the improvised barricade and glided past the Camaro. He headed for the busy intersection of Friendly Avenue and New Garden Road, near the main entrance to the campus of Guilford College. At that intersection, the driver of the civilian car had by now come to a halt in the center lane. In the turn lane on her left sat another civilian car, containing a woman and a child.

There was no longer any pretense of organized tactics. The police were now simply trying to stop Fritz any way they could. Next to try his luck was Officer Spainhour, who gunned his Mustang. Once again, the hapless Officer Dennis was in the way. He swerved to avoid being hit by the Mustang and his car went into a skid. Dennis saw that he was sliding toward the left side of Fritz's Blazer. He first saw Fritz Klenner's arm, then the ominous muzzle of a 9mm Uzi submachine gun. Flames danced from the muzzle, and a torrent of heavy slugs rained down on Dennis's car. And on Dennis.

As he later described it, it was "like being struck with a sledge-hammer." Two rounds from Fritz's Uzi hit Dennis's body. The first one plowed into his armored vest at a spot on the upper-right side of his chest. The second slug missed the armor, but was miraculously deflected by his belt buckle. Dennis lay stunned, in great pain, and radioed weakly for help.

Meanwhile, Fritz came to a halt behind the civilian car stopped in the center lane at the New Garden Road intersection. A second later, Spainhour's Mustang crashed into the civilian vehicle. Fritz calmly turned around and blasted the Mustang with a long ripping burst from his Uzi. Eight bullets struck the car. Spainhour jumped out and pumped a few rounds at Fritz with his pistol. The driver of the civilian car, a by-now thoroughly terrified young woman named Debbie Blanton, cowered in her seat, thinking that Spainhour was about to shoot her.

Nobles wanted a crack at Fritz, too. But when he drew his side-arm, another round from Fritz's Uzi slammed into his weapon and fragmented. Two pieces of the shattered slug buried themselves in his right armpit. Nobles's partner, detective Childers, was hurt as well — Fritz's burst had shattered the windows of their car, and Childers was bleeding from glass cuts. Still, he squeezed off one round in the general direction of Fritz's vehicle, but without noticea-ble results. During the gun battle, Nobles got a good look at Susie. She was "just sitting there, with an expression on her face as if she was waiting for a red light to change."

Meanwhile, all around the busy intersection, shoppers, pedes-trians, and tellers from a nearby bank were diving for cover as the bullets flew. One stray round shattered the window of a car parked in a filling station across the street.The once-peaceful entrance to Guil-ford College, founded in 1837 by the Quakers, was surrounded by smashed cars and bleeding policemen.

Still, the police had Fritz surrounded. Two civilian cars and three police vehicles hemmed him in from all angles. But when Spainhour jumped out to take a shot at Fritz, Spainhour's car, still in gear, rolled forward eight or ten feet and left Fritz a narrow escape route. Even while he was being fired on, Fritz methodically backed up, made an S-turn, got around both civilian cars and Spainhour's banged-up Mustang, calmly turned left onto New Garden Road, and drove away.

Like angry hornets, the command car driven by Travis, then Stur-gill and Gentry, then Fetter's Camaro, all followed the Blazer. Spain-hour tried to fall in behind them, too, but in his excitement he crashed into Debbie Blanton's car for the second time in as many minutes.

Veteran police officers still shake their heads in wonder when the subject of the "intersection shoot-out" comes up. The attempt to surround Fritz at the junction of Friendly Avenue and New Garden Road was not only chaotic, but also against the book. Standard tactical procedure against a heavily armed suspect is to take him as far from a busy intersection as possible. And even if it had worked, if they had boxed him in with their cars, the results would almost certainly have been a nightmare. Fritz might have come out with his guns blazing, and at close quarters an Uzi is a meat-chopper. Worse, he might have reached down and detonated the bomb under the passenger seat. The casualties among both law enforcement personnel and innocent bystanders would have been horrendous — shrapnel would have sprayed over a hundred-yard radius.

When frantic calls went out for back-up units, no one was really sure what was happening. At one point, Greensboro officers being directed to the scene were told to beware of armed suspects in a Camaro and a Mustang. There were armed men in a Camaro and a Mustang, all right, but they were all SBI agents and Forsyth County deputies. It's a miracle the cops didn't start shooting at each other instead of Fritz.

And during all this, the Greensboro police dispatchers were getting radio calls from all their officers who were converging on the scene. The officers were begging, in voices of quiet desperation, for somebody to please tell them just what the hell was going on.

CHAPTER THIRTY-SEVEN

A Hailstorm and a Haydn Mass

After escaping from the Guilford College intersection, Fritz led the growing armada of police cars on a bizarre chase. With Susie and the two boys still in his unscathed Blazer, he drove slowly away from town, always at, and sometimes below, the 35 mph speed limit. He was doing things by the book, putting to work all of those escape-and-evasion tactics he'd read about over the years. One of the rules concerns driving: never blast off like James Bond, since you can lose control of the vehicle that way. And Fritz didn't want to lose control.

At a point where New Garden Road angles off to the right, Fritz pulled the Blazer to a halt, blocking the road in both directions. Then he patiently waited for the pursuing police vehicles to appear around the bend. When they did, he sprayed the leading car of the column with his Uzi. The police returned fire with sidearms and at least one rifle, apparently not inflicting any damage to Fritz's four-by-four. Fritz calmly turned the Blazer away and resumed his drive into the country.

Meanwhile, the police-radio airwaves were filled with confused reports, in which the Blazer was variously described as a "black Mustang," a "red Camaro," and "a truck."

When Fritz reached the intersection of U.S. 220, he turned left onto the two-lane rural highway, leaned over, and fired another burst at the cop cars. By now, the North Carolina Highway Patrol had gotten into the act, as well as the Guilford County Sheriff's Department. Both agencies had units converging on the scene, although there was still enormous confusion over exactly who was being chased, and why, and what they were driving. Still, the lawmen started setting up some roadblocks.

Later, when the police sifted through Fritz's belongings at the apartment, they found a bill of sale for a police scanner. Since the scanner itself was not found in the apartment, it's reasonable to assume that Fritz had it mounted in the Blazer and was listening to all the chaotic radio traffic. It's also possible that he was having the time of his life. If he had ever fantasized about invisible movie cameras rolling on him, this was the big chase scene in the last reel. Before he was through, he would give them something to remember.

A deputy sheriff, Sergeant Hubert Jackson, had been hastily summoned to the scene. He, too, was completely in the dark about the case. He took up a position at the intersection of U.S 220 and State Road 150 when Fritz made a turn onto 150. Jackson would never forget his one telling glimpse of Fritz. Fritz cruised by at an almost contemptuous rate of speed — five or six miles per hour, according to one witness — and as Fritz passed, he turned, looked right at Jackson, and grinned at him.

Long after the event, Jackson was still brooding on that little window of opportunity: "If I had just known more at the time...I had an opportunity there to take him out...If I had just known more at the time...I think I would have shot him."

But Jackson didn't. The moment passed. Fritz continued to drive on at a maddeningly deliberate rate of speed.

A roadblock was now being established farther up Highway 150. It must have been obvious to Fritz, if he was indeed eavesdropping on the radio traffic, that he was approaching the final battle scene. There was no place left to turn except dead-end country lanes and private driveways.

At this point, the nearest law enforcement vehicle was about 200 feet behind the Blazer — a prudent distance, when someone is shooting at you with an automatic weapon. Fritz was still traveling at the speed limit, perhaps a bit slower. He leaned out of the window once more and emptied the Uzi at his pursuers. Then he slowed to about ten miles per hour.

The two cars closest to the Blazer were both being driven by Guilford County deputy sheriffs, who had swung to the head of the line when Fritz had turned onto N.C. 150. Neither Deputy David Thacker, who was closest, nor Deputy Jackson, who was right behind Thacker, could observe any movement in the back seat. Both officers had caught close but fleeting glimpses of Fritz and Susie during the chase. Although the Blazer's windows were tinted, both officers later asserted that the tint was not dark enough to prevent them from seeing inside. They were certain that if either of the two boys in the rear seat had been in a normal upright position, they would have been visible.

Suddenly the Blazer's brake lights came on. Both Thacker and Jackson heard what they later described as "clack-clack" sounds: two distinct reports which were definitely not Uzi shots. But neither deputy observed Fritz firing out of the driver's window at this time. Both men then saw a sudden "commotion" in the Blazer's front seat, a flurry of movement involving both the driver and the passenger. Jackson described it as "a lot of movement." This brief spasm of activity was remarkable because, until then, except for Fritz's over-the-shoulder gunslinging, there had been no discernable movement from anyone else in the Blazer.

When the Blazer's brake lights came on, the lawmen in the closest pursuit cars braced themselves: Fritz seemed ready to come out with all available firepower blazing. And who knew what else he had besides automatic weapons. Antitank rockets?

The Blazer angled to the right side of the highway. Then, at 3:07 p.m., deputy Jackson heard what sounded to him like a hand grenade detonation, and he saw a piece of something fly off the Blazer's roof. Suddenly there was a second explosion. After an intense flash and a "huge boom," an engulfing fireball ripped the top off the Blazer and blew out all its windows. The vehicle disappeared in a cloud of gushing black smoke.

Nobody knows what Fritz's bomb under the passenger seat was made of, but there was a lot of it and it was powerful. A Blazer is a rugged vehicle, yet the blast lifted it as high as the telephone wires on the side of the road and hurled it back down again like a smashed toy. The Blazer slammed into the ground, rolled smoking into a roadside ditch, and then was still. The passenger-side door dangled from a pine tree fifty feet overhead. The rest of the vehicle was a twisted wad of scorched metal.

The stunned officers scrambled out of their cars into the humid afternoon with guns drawn, but there was no fight left in Fritz Klenner. He was still breathing when they got to him, and his body appeared intact, but the force of the explosion had drastically rearranged his internal organs, and his chest cavity was flooding with blood.

Detective Dan Davidson bent over him — hoping, against all the odds, that there might be enough time left for Fritz to tell them something, to confess, apologize, to give some hint of a motive. Fritz made no sound except the wet, phlegmy bleat of a man drowning in his own blood. In a few seconds, he was dead.

Susie had been sitting on top of the bomb. There wasn't much left of her from the waist down, and blood, from the concussion, was seeping from every orifice of her head. The bodies of Jim and John Lynch were found in what was left of the back seat. Between them lay the corpse of one of the big chow dogs. All of the victims were wearing Roman Catholic scapulars and rosary beads. Strung on the scapulars were two prayers: one for salvation, the other for deliverance from purgatory.

A cornucopia of paraphernalia had vomited forth from the Blazer in the explosion: pistols, shotguns, knives, brass knuckles, tarps, flares, tools, C-rations, gas masks, smoke grenades, holsters, climbing ropes, survival manuals, dozens of batteries, even a portable water distillation plant. The whole survivalist smorgasbord. In the middle of all the scattered hardware and survival gear lay a scorched cassette tape blown from the Blazer's in-dash stereo: Franz Joseph Haydn's *Mass in Time of War*.

A few minutes after Fritz died, a vicious black thunderstorm detonated above the wreckage, sending the police scurrying for cover and raking the scene first with torrential rain and then with hail-stones the size of musket balls. When the storm abated, clouds of hot, powder-reeking steam curdled over the pavement, wreathing the wreckage and the corpses, curling softly around the legs of the living.

None of the men who saw that scene has ever been able to forget it. To more than one observer, it seemed as though God Himself had seen fit to express His anger at what had transpired here.

As well He might: Autopsies later revealed that young John and Jim had been given large doses of cyanide poison at some point during the car chase. And just before the explosion, the boys had been shot through the head at point-blank range with Fritz Klenner's 9mm pistol.

Post Mortems

There is one living member of the Klenner family who claims to have been in contact with Fritz from beyond the grave, so I suppose it's possible we may one day be able to read his personal account of what went on in the Blazer on that last ride.

But if you discount that source of information, you just run into a brick wall: We will never, ever, know what was thought or done or said inside that vehicle. It is a void. A legal, moral, and psychological black hole that swallows every attempt to pierce it with light.

One thing that's clear is the connection between Fritz and the cyanide. That's not only logical, it's verifiable. One of his favorite hangouts was the McHargue gun shop in Winston-Salem, where he had managed to convince the McHargues that he really was a Delta Force commando. On at least one occasion, Fritz told them that he and Susie always carried cyanide capsules, in case they should be taken alive by "the enemy."

On July 10, 1985, Mike McHargue told police that Susie had stated that she carried cyanide in her handbag, and that she didn't want to go on living if anything happened to Fritz. Ditto for the two boys. However, when the McHargues were interviewed a few weeks later, on August 2, by a private investigator, their story had changed completely. This time, Steve McHargue, who had been present during the first interview, stated that Susie herself never spoke about the poison and never claimed she had it on her person. Fritz just bragged about how she had it, and those remarks, apparently, were made either when Susie was not with him, or when she was off in another part of the store. So the connection between Susie and the cyanide is at least open to doubt, given the conflicting testimonies.

After establishing the connection between Fritz and the cyanide, after studying everything that happened before that day, and after trying for two solid years to get inside the heads of Fritz and Susie, I'm ready to present two theories:

Theory #1: The Suicide Pact

There is a good deal of circumstantial evidence to suggest that Fritz had not only convinced Susie he was a CIA agent, but also that he might have convinced her that *she* was indirectly working for the Agency, too. He encouraged her to believe that everybody who was after her was after him as well. She was packing a gun, and she knew how to use it. And he had convinced her — there can't be any doubt on this point — that their enemies were close, numerous, and utterly vicious.

Whoever "they" were — some improbable alliance of South American drug dealers, KGB agents, and Tom Lynch's mafia buddies, I suppose — it is entirely possible that Fritz had her believing, on that last day, that "they" had finally come, just as he had been predicting all along.

From Susie's point of view, in the passenger's seat of the Blazer, there was nothing visible to disprove what he was saying. Not until the pursuit was well under way did any marked squad cars join the procession, and they would have been far in the rear, where she couldn't have seen them on most stretches of the route.

All she could see were unmarked vehicles that looked like they came from agency motor pools, with little portable blue gumball lights on top. Maybe he told her these were renegade CIA hit teams or something. Anyhow, there was nothing visible about the pursuing vehicles to identify them as legitimate law enforcement vehicles, if one were heavily programmed to see them as something else.

Also, none of the men shooting at them was in uniform. The only uniformed officer present during the close-range encounters, as far as I've been able to determine, was Tommy Dennis, and even he was driving an unmarked auto. The only time he was close enough for Susie to see him was those few seconds when Fritz was shooting at him, and all of that happened on Fritz's side of the Blazer.

Fritz could have kept up a con almost until the end, when Sheriff's Department and Highway Patrol vehicles started closing in. The radio traffic she might have been hearing over the police scanner wouldn't have enlightened her much, either. She didn't know the code phrases, and there's very little in the content of such transmissions that would enable the untrained ear to identify who is talking to whom.

Given the fatalism inherent in their Armageddon beliefs, and given Susie's occasional hint that she would prefer suicide to living beyond the parameters of those beliefs, a suicide pact between them, one which included the boys, is not beyond the realm of possibility.

Fritz had methodically studied whole encyclopedias of torture and interrogation techniques. Who knows what horrors he had programmed her to expect if "They" took them alive. He probably told her that she would be forced to watch the boys tortured to death. I'm sure he dreamed up some really elaborate and sadistic scenarios proving that death would be preferable.

It is true to the whole secret agent fantasy to have a suicide option — hence, I guess, the cyanide pills. There may have been poison pills for the two of them, too, but they would have been vaporized in the explosion, along with so much else in the Blazer.

If Susie really had been programmed to believe that they were being chased by a team of professional assassins, and really did believe that she and the boys would suffer unspeakable torments if they were taken alive, then she might have believed that giving poison to the boys was a last act of love. It's conceivable that she regarded the coup de grace pistol shots in the same light, although I have not yet reached the point where I can visualize her actually pulling the trigger and watching them get shot. I have less trouble, however, visualizing her allowing Fritz to do it. And he would have done it, too, without a trace of hesitation…as a last dramatic gesture of his "love" for all of them.

Theory #2: Kamikaze

Assuming Fritz had his police scanner on, he probably knew there was a roadblock just a few minutes' drive down Highway 150. His plan could have been to crash the Blazer into that roadblock, detonating the bomb as he did so, and go out in a *Gotterdammerung* blaze of glory, taking as many of the enemy with him as he could. In that case, he would have administered the poison capsules to the boys to "protect" them from the kamikaze run he was planning. Whether Susie really knew what he was giving them, or whether he just told her the pills were powerful tranquilizers, we don't know and never will. It could have been either way, given her state of mind by this time.

Then, of course, you run into this question: How could she just sit there and calmly watch him, a few minutes later, turn around and shoot her children in the face with a high-powered pistol? Maybe she didn't. All the witnesses we interviewed in our private investigation swore that Susie never moved from the time the pursuit started until the explosion. She just sat there staring fixedly ahead. No one has ever come forward to claim that they actually saw her fire a shot. As far as we were able to determine, she never even turned her head to look at the police who were chasing them.

And yet, in the last instant before the explosion, the deputies observed that sudden, wild flurry of movement in the front seat. Maybe she snapped out of it when she realized Fritz was shooting her babies. Maybe she turned on him and tried to rip his eyeballs out, the way any mother would do. Perhaps it was that struggle that prematurely detonated the bomb.

Those are my theories. Take your pick.

I should mention that there's another theory, too. Some months after the shoot-out, the SBI announced that its lab tests indicated Susie had probably fired a weapon. This seemed to support the idea that she had pulled the trigger on her own two sons. It also lent some indirect support to Tom Lynch's and Kentucky policeman Dan Davidson's hypothesis that Susie was really the mastermind behind the debacle all along.

Since the SBI refuses to describe in detail just what kind of tests they ran, let's assume it was their standard powder test, which is called a *dermal nitrate* test. It consists of wiping the back of the hand with hydrochloric acid and then testing the sample for the presence of nitrates, a family of chemicals which are present in all bullet propellants, ancient or modern, since they are an important ingredient in gunpowder.

All that test will tell you is whether or not nitrates are present. It won't tell you where the nitrates came from. There are dozens of other common sources for nitrate besides gunpowder: garden fertilizer, for instance, or camera film. Nitrates are so common, in fact, that most forensic law professors now tell their students that the nitrate test is not the best thing to carry into court, simply because a good defense lawyer can shoot it full of holes.

There is a second, more specialized test, called *neutron activation*. You take the hand-wipings, just as before, and then you have them irradiated. Then you measure the half-life of the isotopes that were created by that exposure to radiation. Most nitrates won't form isotopes at all, but heavy metals, such as beryllium and lead, will. Microscopic particles of those elements remain for a fairly long time in the skin of someone who has fired a pistol. If this test comes out positive, you're in a strong position to make a case that yes, this person recently fired a handgun.

There are problems, however, even with this test. The weapon could have been fired days before the crime. And remember that Susie often did go shooting with Fritz, up in the country near the family farm. Also, there are certain kinds of ammo, especially fully jacketed military ammo of the kind Fritz preferred to shoot, which simply don't leave much of a heavy metal trace.

If the SBI did perform a neutron activation test, then maybe I'll have to revise my theories. But the SBI isn't talking. And even if they did such a test, it would be the first time it's ever happened in my experience as a trial lawyer, because the SBI is not normally set up to run such a specialized procedure.

Also, frankly, the SBI lab does not have the highest reputation among law enforcement agencies and lawyers in North Carolina. I remember reading a story in the papers about two young men who had done several months of hard time in jail because the SBI lab fouled up a simple drug analysis.

Just as there can be no excuses for the incredible snafu of the arrest attempt itself, there can be no excuses for the slovenly procedures after the Blazer blew up. There were no fingerprints lifted from the weapons on the scene — not even the 9mm pistol that killed the children. The officers handled the weapons as they found them, utterly ruining any chance to determine if Susie had indeed fired the gun that killed her sons.

Also, the first statement about the powder residue that was issued by the SBI was very strange. The tests were "inconclusive," they said, because there were residual chemicals all over her exposed flesh from the bomb blast. Then, without blushing, the SBI claimed it was impossible to determine what kind of bomb Fritz had used because "the rain had washed away all traces" of the very same residue, a little contradiction that has never been explained. Then, later, they implied — without ever detailing their test results — that they did find residue on Susie that was consistent with her having fired a gun.

It was consistent with her having fired a gun. It was also consistent with her having been blown up. The bottom line is that no systematic attempt was ever made to learn, from the remains of the Blazer and its occupants, whatever could have been learned by a first-rate forensic lab. It's as though the SBI was in a hurry to close its books on this mess and forget about it. Of course, when you look at how they screwed up, that's an understandable attitude. But forgive me for not being too sympathetic about it personally.

About six months after everything blew up, I was contacted by a gun-control organization and asked if they could use my name and my family's story in their advertising campaign. Not wishing to be a hypocrite, I turned them down, pointing out that the murders would have taken place even if every handgun in America had been confiscated years ago. The man we had been dealing with was not your ordinary drunk waving a Saturday Night Special in a pool hall. He was a man who had devoted years of his life to the study of mayhem and killing, and he went at his killing coldly, methodically, and without mercy or remorse. He didn't even need guns. He knew a hundred ways to kill.

The night after my parents and grandmother were killed on Valley Road, I'd recovered my senses enough to figure out who and what we were dealing with. My wife Alice and I contacted several friends and neighbors who bravely offered to keep our children, making it hard for anyone to track them down. We gratefully accepted this arrangement. One of the things that frightened us both the most was the fact that, if things had just gone a little differently that weekend, our oldest daughter might have been staying at Nana's, too, on the night Fritz decided to pay his visit. He would have killed our daughter just as coldly as he killed everybody else.

Of course, the entire surviving family had told the police everything we knew and everything we suspected. But, as a lawyer, I knew it would probably take several days for them to get enough evidence together to issue an arrest warrant that would stick. In situations like this there's really very little the police can offer you in terms of actual protection. What they can do, and often do very well indeed, is avenge your death, but that's pretty cold comfort.

There was a frightening window of time, then, between the Valley Road murders and the day the cops felt ready to make their move.

During that time, I would be my family's main line of defense. I had sold most of my guns a year before, but I armed myself with what I had, a 12-gauge shotgun loaded with No. 4 buckshot. I was prepared to kill him with it. I was even turning over plans in my mind about how I could lure him to my house and simply bushwhack the bastard when he stepped out of his Blazer.

I might have faced prosecution for it, but I knew a couple of not-too-shabby defense lawyers. The point is that prosecution was the furthest thing from my mind at that moment. I was convinced that Fritz meant to wipe out Susie's entire family and that I was next on the hit list. And right after the protection of my wife and children, my main priority was to keep breathing myself. When I mentioned all this to the gun-control people, I could feel their reaction. They were thinking: Ah-hah, so you had a gun and you sat there waiting for a chance to kill a man with it. Doesn't that make you like him?

No, I'm sorry, but it doesn't. I live here. I only wanted to stop this one man, but he was ready to kill anybody and everybody who got in his way. We're not talking about some deprived, drug-addled street kid from the slums. We're talking about a cunning, educated adult whose highest ambition in life, after he found out he didn't have what it takes to be a doctor, was to become the Terminator. And, just like the killer-robot in that movie, once these people get started, the only way to stop them is to pull out their plug.

Not too long after my chat with the gun-control lobbyists, a phalanx of fundamentalists descended on a supine North Carolina state legislature in Raleigh and got a law passed which made it a crime to view an X-rated videotape in the privacy of one's own home. Those same extremists have managed to get *Playboy* and *Penthouse* yanked out of the curb markets in many places, too.

Well, the books that taught Fritz Klenner how to kill people are still openly for sale at the surplus stores where he used to buy his survivalist gear. You can go in there and see fourteen-year-olds with their noses buried in this stuff. Here are some titles jotted down at random: *How to Kill* (that one comes in six volumes — very thorough — and has been banned from open sale in Canada); *The Brassknuckle Bible*; *Principles of the Quick Kill*; *The Manual of*

eld Interrogation (this one teaches you how to fill a sock with wet
ud and beat information out of prisoners); *The CIA Explosives
anual*; *The Sabotage Manual of the OSS*; *The Handbook of Auto-
atic and Concealable Firearms*. The titles just go on, rack after
ck, in that same vein, fueling the bang-bang fantasies of every
happy adolescent who dreams about being Rambo and never hav-
g to take any crap from anybody ever again.

I refuse to argue for legislation to ban those books, even though I
ill always associate them with the lunatic who decimated my
mily. The price we pay for living in a free society is that we have to
it up with being exposed to things we find personally offensive. If
u're going to ban *Penthouse*, then you should also ban *Soldier of
rtune* — the obscenity quotient is about the same in both maga-
nes — or you should ban neither. And I can assure you that nothing
any X-rated video you will ever see, *nothing*, could be any more
scene than the sight of my sister's body lying in pieces in the
eeds alongside Highway 150.

What happened to my family was Biblical in its extremity, and it
s given me some inkling of how the survivors of the Holocaust
ust feel. The Newsoms have lost four generations of people. Aside
om my own wife and children, the closest relatives I have left in
e world are aunts and uncles.

Surviving is better than the alternative, of course, but it also has
penalties, as anyone who has lived through a plane crash or com-
t can tell you. You wonder why you weren't swept away in the
me tidal wave that took everyone else, and you feel vaguely guilty
neath your gratitude to whatever power or random factor it was
at saved you. There are days when depression settles in like a
terfront fog, days when I wonder if it's worth the effort even to try
accomplish anything, days when I simply have no enthusiasm for
e itself.

You keep going, of course, and time numbs the edges a little. But
weighs you down to realize that you'll never, ever, be entirely free
what happened.

I miss them all: Mom, Nana, and Susie, too…but as I approach
ddle age, I think I feel the loss of my father the most keenly. He

had already passed through these years, and I could have enjoyed the comfort of his presence, could have turned to him for the kind of guidance only your dad can give you.

Since we decided to keep this house, we've tried to keep the gardens going with the same care and devotion and attentiveness that he had for them — not always with the best results, I'm afraid. I don't have his knack for it.

Oh, Lord, how he loved those rose bushes! I can't help it, but every year, when they first burst into bloom, and the air in the yard grows all sweet and rich with their aroma, I have to bite back the impulse to pick up the phone, call my father, and tell him that his roses are still beautiful.

Apocalypse, Wow!

"Ezekiel 38 and 39 say that Gog, a northern power, will invade Israel. Gog must be Russia. Most of the prophecies that had to be fulfilled before Armageddon can come, have come to pass. Ezekiel said that fire and brimstone will be rained upon the enemies. That must mean that they'll be destroyed by nuclear weapons."

— Ronald Wilson Reagan, in a statement to the President Pro Tem of the California State Senate, 1971.

"We were talking about the fact that the Middle East, according to the Bible, would be the place where Armageddon would start . . . ."

— Ronald Wilson Reagan, quoted in *The New York Times*, October 19, 1981.

"Believe me... these prophecies [the Book of Revelations*] certainly describe the times we're going through."* — Ronald Wilson Reagan, in the *Jerusalem Post*, 1983.

Fritz Klenner's obsession with Armageddon was not an isolated trait within the Klenner family, but part of a large and growing cultural phenomenon in the 1970s and 1980s. It is important to understand this, because Fritz's belief in the imminence of civilization's collapse was a prime justification in his own mind for the worst of his actions.

And to understand what happened in the minds of Fritz Klenner and Susie Newsom Lynch after they came together, you must understand how his belief in Armageddon led him to construct, and her to embrace, a psychotic fantasy that destroyed two families.

Fritz's belief that Armageddon would take place on or before the year 2000 may well have been implanted by his father, but that belief is far from unique to the Klenners. And in one sense, Fritz and Doc were right. The years between now and 2000 are going to be increasingly dangerous, if only because so many thousands of people have attached such a heavy weight of symbolism to that date.

History does not, on the evidence, divide itself conveniently into 1000-year cycles. But mankind continues to attach enormous symbolic and emotional significance to the passage of each millennium. The approach of the year 1000 was viewed with awe and consternation by every nation which measured time by the same yardstick. Omens and portents abounded, prophets did a booming business, nations were turbulent, and fanatical sects appeared all over Europe and the Middle East, preaching a host of eschatologies.

Their message was, at bottom, always the same: The end-time was at hand, and the millennium would be a watershed in the destiny of humanity.

Untidy thing that it is, history did not oblige. It would be another four centuries until the Renaissance.

And now, once again, as the year 2000 approaches, a millennial fever is sweeping the land, and with it, much talk about the end of time. But things are different now than they were in tenth-century Europe. A thousand years ago, when the imminence of apocalypse was thundered by clerics, prophets, and madmen, their effect on the workaday world around them was localized and limited by the difficulties of communication.

In contemporary America, the horrors of Armageddon are the stuff of best-sellers. Armageddon permeates the sermons of dozens of Bible-pounding evangelists whose television programs influence millions. And the common, shared awareness that the end of the world really could happen — any day, in the space of a few isotope-drenched hours — lends even the most extravagant prophecies a sense of plausibility never attached to their medieval counterparts.

The citizen of tenth-century Europe could conceive of the end only in terms of the hand of God. The citizen of late twentieth-century America can conceive, all too easily, of the hand of man, poised over the infamous button, as the agency of ultimate doom.

For the first time in history, a generation has reached middle age having lived its entire time on earth with the certain knowledge that civilization is balanced on a knife's edge. The long-term psychological and social effects of living with The Bomb have gone beyond simple individual fear. Like diseased tendrils, the existential uncertainty, and the overriding sense of sheer helplessness, have branched out through every aspect of our society. This dread is always somewhere in our minds. Occasionally it emerges in odd, troubling ways.

Perhaps the most troubling symptom is that thousands of people have begun to gravitate from preparing for the holocaust to actually wishing for it. For a surprising number of people, this lust-for-apocalypse has become the sole focus of their zeal. Their commitment to a sectarian madness has finally come to light, like a rotted, long-growing fungus, as the saddest product of five decades of nuclear fear. It is called survivalism.

Of course, under certain circumstances, survival preparations are not demented but rather prudent. If you live on the Atlantic coast in the route of the great hurricanes, it makes good sense to have emergency supplies, an evacuation plan, and a good first-aid kit. If you live in a tornado zone and build a stout, well-stocked shelter in your basement, you are not acting like a paranoid sociopath, but like a sensible person.

Fifteen years ago, when you spoke of "survivalists," you were talking about a loose population of individualists who stocked food, water, and a few guns just in case the Russians invaded or the economy collapsed — a sort of gloomy reprise of the family bomb-shelter craze of the Fifties.

We all have different ways of coping with the accumulated stress of nuclear anxiety. If you live in a big city, or near what is called a "primary target" (a missile silo complex, a big naval base, any major government installation, and so forth), maybe your best bet is simply to hope for an instantaneous death close to ground-zero. Millions of people have rationalized their position that way, shrugged, tried to put the nuclear terror out of their minds, and gone on with their everyday lives.

But if you live in a small community in, say, rural Montana, away from any missile silos and out of the projected fallout patterns, it's not unreasonable to figure that, with the help of a trusty rifle and a year's supply of freeze-dried food, you can ride out the catastrophe.

This is what you might call the "small-s" survivalist — just your average person, interested as we all are in self-preservation, not in any nutty political agenda. This old-fashioned "mountain man" breed of survivalist at least appears to embody certain traditional and very appealing American virtues: self-sufficiency, individual initiative, and a creative ability to live off the land. As a bonus, this approach even has all the virtues of solitary communion with nature. Sort of like Thoreau with a Winchester.

The problem is that the line between a rational attitude toward personal survival and irrational, extremist zeal has become very fine indeed. The very act of drawing up an elaborate plan for armed personal survival positions you within an antisocial matrix of ideas and behavior patterns.

If you survive the holocaust by virtue of your foresight, you will inevitably run head-on into the problem of what to do about the others: the majority of happenstance survivors who were not prepared for the crisis and who will be wandering in dazed, irradiated, desperate hordes across the smoldering, ravaged countryside, looking for the very things you have and they need, such as food, shelter, and medicine. You can't take care of them, feed them, or dress their wounds. You really have only two choices: give them what you've got or kill them to stop them from taking it.

Thus, the unpleasant corollary to personal survival schemes is always the likelihood of waging war against your fellow Americans. It is at this point in the political and moral continuum that small-s survivalism mutates into Survivalism.

Survivalism with a capital *S* is really a phenomenon of the Eighties, a period that has been so rife with Armageddonists and their various harangues that some sociologists have dubbed it The Doomsday Decade. In the middle-third of that decade, something new and dangerous loomed into the public eye for the first time: the specter of armed, organized, ultra-violent hate-groups in the heartland of America. These were people who were not merely waiting for The Bomb to fall, but who were actively pursuing an agenda of robbery, assassination, and intimidation, all designed to hasten the day when the bombs would fall. This would be a day which would signal that the time had come to implement their screwball ideologies in large parts of the nation. Power would shift to the powerless.

The incident that brought these groups out from under their respective rocks and into the light of national scrutiny was the submachine-gun slaying of Denver talk-show host Alan Berg. The men responsible for stalking and ambushing Berg were discovered to be members of an organization known as The Silent Brotherhood (*Bruder Schweigen* to its members, who prefer, for ideological reasons, the German title), but more widely known to the media simply as The Order. It was from the trial of Berg's killers that the public got its first really close look at the new Survivalist Right.

What emerged was a picture of a movement comprised of people who do not — unlike the earlier generation of individual survivalists — simply want to ride out Armageddon. Instead, they actually seek to employ Armageddon to their own fanatical ends. Their belief in its imminence is simply a tool to further their racial and political ideals. Far from hating The Bomb, these people see nuclear war as a convenient means of "cleansing" society of Jews, blacks, homosexuals, and "mongrels" (people of racially mixed origins).

More specifically, the new Survivalist Right is a loose affiliation of neo-Nazis, religious extremists, and those secretive heartland anarchists who call themselves the Posse Comitatus. Each band has its own particular ideological axe to grind, but there is a common political philosophy that unites all of these sects, from the Fundamentalist Apocalyptics to the Aryan Nations: the belief that the entire apparatus of the U.S. government has been suborned by a sinister cabal of Jewish bankers, masters of the Illuminati, and a random grouping of moderate-to-liberal diplomats dubbed Trilateralists. The master plan of these hidden power-mongers and string-pullers calls for the gradual corruption of traditional American values, the surreptitious gutting of the American economy (sometime in the late Sixties, according to Survivalist Right mythology, the Jews secretly removed all the gold from Fort Knox), the spreading of discontent throughout the nonwhite urban poor, and then — when the time is ripe — the triggering of a nuclear war.

To most of us, these are extreme, if not downright silly, paranoid fantasies. Yet, they are given credibility by the less violent but generically similar views that pour from the media into the minds of many people who are already — thanks to the confusions, fears, and economic uncertainties of the times we live in — predisposed to believe that somebody, somewhere, is conspiring against them and their way of life.

Every day, televangelists on our tubes drive home the message that Armageddon is right around the corner and that when it comes, the world will be cleansed of atheists, pornographers, abortion clinics, and Dan Rather. Reinforcement has even come from the highest office in the land, such as when President Ronald Reagan talked of Biblical prophecies, and when he appointed as his secretary of the interior a man who tried, until he was forced out of office, to open up the national park lands to commercial development out of a sincere belief that ours will be the last generation before the apocalypse.

Extremist views also gain credibility in the heartland as family after family is driven into bankruptcy by a system of enticing government loans that, for too many farmers, have become a vicious snare. Family farms are going under. A way of life is dying that has fueled the American tradition for generations. People are being driven off their land and there is nowhere for them to go. The unskilled blue-collar jobs in the cities, which traditionally offered a refuge for farm boys in hard times, don't pay enough to live on.

It is these people, fundamentally decent and freedom loving, who are targeted by the new generation of hate-mongers. When anti-Semitic groups like the Liberty Lobby and the American Populist Party tell them that Zionist bankers are manipulating the currency, subverting the Federal Reserve System, and seeking to wipe out the small-scale family farm, some of these downtrodden people are ready to listen. From believing that Jewish bankers really do control the money system, it is but a short leap, for desperate minds, to the monstrous proposition that the Nazi Holocaust never really happened, but was only a brilliant propaganda scheme designed to generate sympathy for Israel in the late 1940s. And anyone who crosses that intellectual line is ready for any kind of lunatic theory that comes along, even Lyndon LaRouche's contention that the British royal family is the head of all international dope-smuggling operations.

There is also a common thread of theology binding together these diverse hate groups. It is called Identity Christianity, and its proponents can expound on its beliefs with a subtlety that staggers the rational mind. The hate-mongering preachers are, if possible, even more dangerous than the openly rabid Jew-haters, for their very mastery of pseudo-scientific jargon convinces some people that beneath so much intellectual smoke there must burn the fires of truth.

As Byzantine as some of the Identity doctrines are, the sect's basic theology is chillingly easy to follow. It goes like this: The chosen people of God are not the same as the people who are called Jews today; they are in fact the white people who first settled America — good, hearty, Anglo-Saxon stock. The real Jews, so Identity preachers argue, were the ancestors of those who today describe themselves as Aryans. These are the chosen people about whom the Bible really speaks, not the Semitic impostors who call themselves Jews today. These "white Jews" left the Holy Land about a thousand years before the birth of Christ and migrated to England and Northern Europe, where they became Danes, Angles, Jutes, Teutons, and so forth.

As for those who call themselves "Jews" today, well, they are the seed of Satan, planted in Eve at the same time God planted the seed of the white race. They are the descendants of Cain, the wicked son of Adam, who became the Central Asian tribe called Khazars (an Identity corruption of Ashkenazim). They snuck back into the Holy

Land long after the real tribes of Israel had split for the Nordic climes.

According to this philosophy, Jefferson, Adams, Washington, and the rest of the Founding Fathers were actually elders of a tribe of True Jews called the Mannaseh who were sent, on God's direct orders, to found the United States. God gave them the Declaration of Independence and the Constitution in the same direct way He gave Moses the Ten Commandments. But generations of immigrant Khazars, now calling themselves Jews, have amended the Constitution in ways that will weaken and eventually destroy the nation's fiber, such as giving the vote to women and blacks. The income tax and the Federal Reserve System were other triumphs of this same hidden Zionist cabal. Today, they also control the universities, the medical establishment, the courts, and what Identity believers often refer to as the "Jews-media."

There is a name for this hidden government: ZOG (Zionist Occupational Government), and the Survivalist Right sees its hand in every element of society. Those missing children whose heartrending photos stare at you from the milk cartons in your grocery cart? They were stolen by Jewish agents during Purim and Passover, and used in blood sacrifice rituals in hidden temples.

Along with that old medieval cliche, the Survival Right also assigns blame to the Jews for the Black Plague, the slaughter of the Christians by Nero, the downfall of Napoleon, and the Bolshevik revolution. As for the connection between Zionism and Communism, the fact that Karl Marx was born a Jew is all the Identity Christians need to prove intimate collusion between the nefarious elders of Zion and the worldwide Red conspiracy.

If this is not enough to make your mind reel, consider a further aspect of the Identity religion. Like Fritz Klenner's personal creed, it encourages a mind-set in which the individual true believer perceives certain crimes as virtuous acts. Adherents are proud of ideas and deeds which would, in most of us, elicit feelings of guilt and shame. It is a sociopathic religion, and it comes complete with a set of "virtues" that are to ordinary morals what its "theology" is to normal Christianity.

Every Survivalist has a favorite end-time scenario, but there are four which are plausible enough to have won wide "constituencies":

Socio-economic collapse. This is now the odds-on favorite among hard-core Survivalists, having replaced nuclear war as the most popular apocalypse sometime early in the Reagan administration. In this scenario, the American money system just collapses. Any number of things could trigger it: inflation, a stock market crash, an interrupted oil supply. After it happens, all essential services and normal systems of food distribution will collapse. In a kind of domino progression, these disruptions would trigger massive urban riots, followed by the breakdown of law enforcement and health services, which could lead to the outbreak of widespread epidemics.

Some form of the socio-economic scenario appears to have been Doc Klenner's favorite; Fritz's, too.

Nuclear war. Still a big favorite, with a long tradition. It could be started when an international poker game gets out of hand; when a few well-placed terrorist devices are triggered; when some pushy little Third World country decides to punish a traditional enemy; when a president or group of generals goes crazy; when a limited conventional war escalates beyond control. Take your pick.

Natural disasters. Of the various Horsemen of the Apocalypse who ride under this banner, Famine is probably given the heaviest odds. What happened in Ethiopia in the mid-1980s could happen again, elsewhere, and profoundly destabilize the world economy. This scenario is usually accompanied in Survivalist literature by visions of starving Third World hordes flooding the globe like locusts, devouring every "have" country in their path. The dissipation of the ozone layer is also coming up fast in popularity, as frightening projections and satellite photographs gradually make their impact on the public. Surely, a sudden melt-down of polar ice would have nearly as severe an effect, worldwide, as a middling-sized nuclear exchange. The long overdue Big One along the San Andreas Fault would be a regional, rather than a national catastrophe, but for the folks living in the affected area, the results would be very serious, and survivalist skills would surely come into play until order was restored.

Pestilence. A Biblical favorite, given new vigor by the AIDS epidemic. Medically speaking, there is no real reason to discount a resurgence, in possibly mutated and more resistant form, of the Black Death — the germs still flourish in the rat populations of our cities. As one Survivalist classic puts it (*Life After Doomsday*, by Bruce D. Clayton, Ph.D.): "...one can't help but wonder how long it will be before an illegal alien with a fleabite sneaks into the barrios of Los Angeles and then refuses to see a doctor when the coughing and fever set in. He'll cough, and his friends will cough, and their friends will cough . . . ."

If the AIDS epidemic proves anything, it is that deadly new diseases can arise for which science has no easy fix. It is fortunate that the disease has such a long, slow, incubation period. For something such as Lassa Fever (a totally new and extremely lethal disease which appeared in Nigeria in 1969, and which kills its victims in a matter of days or even hours) the prospect of infection being spread all over the world by jet airplane passengers is a chilling possibility indeed. Fortunately, Lassa Fever has proven to be not very infectious, but that was just our good luck. Given modern transportation, a deadly virus that suddenly emerges in Botswanaland could be spreading through New York in a matter of hours. In that sense, we are today even more vulnerable to epidemic than the Black Plague victims of the Middle Ages, who at least had time to move if they knew the disease was spreading in their direction.

Fritz Klenner absorbed all of these ideas from his environment. In some ways, potential doom became more real to him than quotidian reality. Such a long, enraptured contemplation of doom cannot but have an unsettling effect on the mind. As Nietzsche cautioned many years ago, do not look too long into the Abyss, or the Abyss will starting looking into you.

What Fritz didn't get from his father, by way of apocalyptic lore, he absorbed from the Survivalist literature. That genre is truly vast, and it ranges from crudely written screeds that might well have come from the pages of *Die Sturmer* (such as *Henry Kissinger — Agent of Doom* and *The Plot Against Doctor Mengele*), to sophisticated how-to-make-bombs-and-kill-people manuals, to the macho posturing and breast-beating of *Soldier of Fortune* magazine, one of Fritz Klenner's favorites.

Fritz was also extremely well-read in the fiction of Survivalism, a genre that, at its best moments, barely deserves to be called "subpulp." Since 1980, a huge library of these post-holocaust adventure yarns has accumulated in the catalogs of some paperback publishers. Usually, the books are published as series, with titles such as *The Killmaster*, *Endworld*, and *The Last Ranger*.

The plot normally focuses on the post-apocalypse adventures of a rugged, well-prepared, Ramboesque hero as he pursues some objective through an environment that has all the trappings of a Mad Max movie. Politics, except for generic anti-Communism, are kept to a minimum. The emphasis is on bang-bang, military hardware, and the deployment of arcane Survivalist expertise. There is action every four or five pages, and even the most obtuse reader can quickly see that, if you substitute the cliches of sex for the cliches of weaponry and mayhem, these books follow the classic formulas of hardcore pornography.

Throughout these narratives, the heros dispatch dozens, sometimes hundreds, of enemies. Not once, in any of these books, does the protagonist experience guilt or remorse at the slaughter he is called upon to commit. Instead, he revels in it, and in the details and nuances of his firepower and the effect it has on human flesh. Indeed, the only really imaginative writing to be found in most of these books is the prose employed to describe the effects of firepower on one's enemies (who are not described as "men" at all, but as "bad asses," "hard cases," or just "slimebags"; how can you experience guilt for killing a "slimebag"?):

"An M16A2 head-shot tore away the commando's skull, spilling red cauliflower salad across the glass-littered dashboard."

"A hail of 9mm zappers destroyed the shotgunner from the waist down, tearing away his stomach, bladder, genitals, small intestines, kneecaps, and all the arteries and muscle tissue over, under, and in between."

"Flame belched from the Uzi's maw. The leftmost half of Badass Two's face vaporized in a bloody cloud. The shattered cheekbones gleamed jaggedly. The left eye popped in its socket, hanging from a bundle of twisted white nerve fibers while brain-matter slopped out through the empty hole . . . . "

These excerpts are from a popular Survivalist series called *The Phoenix* ostensibly written by someone named David Alexander, who dedicates these sensitive volumes to the Special Forces (Green Beret veterans are flattered, no doubt). Alexander is typical of the writers who pander to the machine-gun opera audience. People don't just shoot guns in his books, they shoot particular *kinds* of guns. Every time a round is fired, the weapon, ammunition, and customized modifications are described fully, often in such acronym-laden detail that the sentences trip over themselves: "The girl opened fire with her MAC 10 420 ACP SMG equipped with a SIONIC type noise suppressor attachment for silent killing and forty-round clips that could be discharged by blowback compression in just under thirty seconds."

From violence-porn to mercenary memoirs, Fritz Klenner steeped himself in these images. He also read and re-read a work of fiction that has become the *Moby Dick* of Survivalist literature: *The Turner Diaries*, by a former physics professor named William Pierce. This book is to political extremism what the works of the Marquis de Sade are to the fringes of sexual behavior.

Written around 1970, *The Turner Diaries* recounts the heroic struggles of a Survivalist named Earl Turner, a man who has spent years preparing to resist the machinations of the worldwide Zionist conspiracy. In Turner's America, the Jews have openly seized power. Laws have been passed which force white people to marry racially inferior partners, raising terrible havoc with the gene pool and flooding the streets with drooling, retarded mulattos. New banking laws make it easy and cheap for mixed couples to obtain houses in what used to be all-white neighborhoods. A law called the Cohen Act makes it illegal to own firearms, and goon squads of blacks now roam through the white enclaves, tearing up peoples' houses looking for hidden guns. And the Supreme Court, needless to say, promulgates outrageous laws that permit sexual exploitation of white women by "black bucks."

Pierce's hero joins an underground resistance movement called The Order and wages urban guerilla war by robbing banks and Jewish businesses. The Order systematically and pitilessly assassinates black and Jewish politicians, media intellectuals, and law enforcement personnel (one man Fritz knew bragged that his most vivid personal fantasy is to kill a cop someday). Turner goes on numerous missions which involve tracking down and killing homosexuals, rabbis, and young women with black boyfriends.

Turner and his comrades carry out a plot to ruin the national economy by flooding the market with counterfeit money. At the novel's end, Turner goes out in a mushroom cloud of glory while attacking ZOG military headquarters (formerly the Pentagon) with a tactical nuke.

If this bare-bones outline of Pierce's pornographically violent novel strikes you as just a whacked-out Jew-baiting version of the elephantine miniseries *Amerika*, be assured that to thousands of people on the Survivalist Right, *The Turner Diaries* is gospel, a work of true prophecy. And for one particularly savage group, the novel was an actual blueprint for mayhem.

Members of The Order used *The Turner Diaries* to wage their private war against ZOG. They even called it "ZOG" during their reign of terror in the Pacific Northwest in the early 1980s.

They robbed banks and armored cars, set off bombs in porn theaters, masterminded two counterfeit schemes (one of them embarrassingly dumb and the other quite sophisticated), and they killed or wounded a fair number of people. They also distributed something like $800,000 in stolen funds to various like-minded hate groups throughout rural America. The money was used to buy vast quantities of arms and ammunition and to establish a sophisticated computer telecommunications network which is still functioning and serves as a national bulletin board for the Survival Right.

Fritz Klenner drifted from one group of gun-nuts to the next, soaking up all this background noise and mixing it with the indoctrination he'd already received at home from his father. It's not known if he ever formally joined any of the more organized movements, but it seems reasonably certain that some of the people he hung out with were associated with the now-infamous White Patriot Party.

There are a lot of individuals like Fritz in the ranks of the movement, people who drift from one organization to the next, feeding their hate and fueling their fantasies. The Survivalist movement as a whole has proven to be an exceptionally fertile incubator for a number of characters who take their cues from its member groups, but who, for personal reasons, prefer to act alone. These people are, in fact, common enough to have acquired their own label within the movement: the Survivalists refer to them as "lone wolves."

In addition to Fritz Klenner, here are some of the other, better known lone wolves:

David and Doris Young. On May 16, 1985, the Youngs drove up to an elementary school in the little community of Cokeville, Wyoming, and took 167 people hostage (150 of them children) with a bomb made of two containers full of gasoline. While Doris Young stood by with her hand on the detonating device, David carried in some of the 55 weapons he had brought in their van (some of which, after much FBI work, would be traced back to the arsenals of various Posse Comitatus hideouts). After herding the hostages into a classroom, David Young grandly informed them that they had been chosen to "found a new race." He then went into the school office and phoned in his ransom demands: $300 million and a chat with President Reagan.

David Young had become convinced, through his reading of Survivalist Right literature, that the white race was doomed, because of integration and intermarriage, to mongrelize into a race of "mud people." The Youngs wanted to take their ransom money, buy an island, sequester the children, and use them to develop a new, pure, Aryan race.

They never got a chance. Distracted by a first-grade teacher who was complaining about a headache, Doris lost her grip on the detonator mechanism. The gasoline bomb exploded in her face like a cloud of napalm. Hideously seared by the blast, Doris lay convulsing and screaming when David ran into the room. After putting her out of her misery with two shots, David turned the pistol on himself and put a .44-caliber slug through his skull.

Seventy-eight of the hostages were burned, 21 of them seriously. The psychological scars suffered by the surviving children are incalculable.

David Lewis Rice. On Christmas Eve 1985, in Seattle, Rice dressed in camouflage clothing and entered the home of Charles Goldmark, a prominent and widely respected liberal lawyer. After subduing the family with a realistic toy pistol, Rice handcuffed Goldmark, his wife Annie, and their two sons, Colin (ten) and Derek (twelve). Then he bludgeoned and hacked them to death with a steam iron and a carving knife.

When apprehended, Rice told interviewers that he did it because he had read a diatribe by Survivalist pundit Colonel Jack Mohr which convinced him that there was an army of Chinese Communists poised just across the Canadian border, and another army of North Koreans biding their time just over the Mexican border, waiting for an invasion order to be given by the Federal Reserve Board.

The connection between this hypothesis and the Goldmark family existed only in the twisted depths of David Rice's brain, of course. The point to be made by this horror story is that Rice saw himself not as having committed a hideous and pointless crime, but as having participated in one of the early skirmishes of Armageddon. "It is war," he has said repeatedly to interviewers, in his quiet, toneless voice, "and I am a soldier, and sometimes soldiers have to kill."

A psychologist who participated in Rice's trial laid the blame for his delusions right on the doormat of the Survivalist movement, pointing out that while David Rice was clearly a disturbed individual, the ideas which spurred him to his acts were not dredged up from the murk of his own psyche. "Mr. Rice did not cook up this stuff by himself, out of touch with society...Rather, he belonged to a subgroup of individuals who believed in and supported those ideas. In fact, these people validated these ideas as rational and important. In this regard, I think these people share at least a moral responsibility for what happened."

Leonard Lake and Charles Ng. After constructing a textbook Survivalist bunker in California's isolated Calavaras County (once the heart of Gold Rush country), Lake and Ng kidnapped neighbors, old friends, casual acquaintances, and total strangers, took them to the soundproofed "bunker," and auditioned them for a fantasy army of "Aryan Warriors" and female "seed-carriers" which the two men planned to lead after Armageddon.

Evidently, none of those abducted met the high standards of physical excellence and racial purity demanded by the two erstwhile field marshals, for nobody who entered their fallout-proof compound came out alive. The male prisoners were summarily killed and disposed of in the woods.

The women, however, were treated somewhat more elaborately. They were subjected to stringent sexual bondage, then forced to engage in every conceivable sort of sex act with the two Survivalists. When their captors wearied of them, they were tortured to death, often with severe mutilation. Some of these acts were recorded, in color and with sound, on a video camera hidden behind a one-way mirror. Hundreds of still photos were also taken and neatly kept in scrapbooks.

Lake was arrested over a minor altercation with a store clerk. A routine vehicle check revealed he was driving a car that belonged to a San Francisco man who had been reported missing a year earlier. An assassin-style pistol, complete with silencer, was found in Lake's trunk. Confronted with these anomalies, Lake requested pencil and paper, wrote a farewell note to his parents, and swallowed a cyanide pill that he had secreted in a compartment in his belt buckle. Ng was arrested after fleeing to Canada.

When investigators explored the chamber of horrors in Calavaras County, they not only discovered the stomach-turning videotapes, but also located four cremation pits deep in the woods where victims had been disposed of — some of them, evidently, after dismemberment. More than two dozen plastic bags of human debris were recovered, including fingernails, skull fragments, finger bones, and baby teeth. No one knows how many people died so that these two harbingers of Armageddon could act out their fantasies. Estimates run as high as twenty-five.

According to the United States Civil Rights Commission, there were 49 incidents of anti-Semitic violence in America in 1979; in

1985, there were 638. According to the Justice Department, there may be as many as 500,000 illegal automatic weapons in the hands of Survivalist groups and gun fetishists who incline toward a similar philosophy.

It is probably going to get worse before the year 2000 actually comes and takes some of the wind out of the sails of these groups. With every year that passes, the minds of the Survivalists come under increasing psychic tension from two directions.

First, like slow drops of corrosive acid, every year that goes by without Armageddon wears out the nerves and restraints of these people. To become a proficient Survivalist, a person must make a drastic commitment of time, money, and energy. The basic recommended arsenal for a single Survivalist (assault rifle/street-sweeper shotgun/.45-caliber or 9mm automatic pistol) costs as much as a good used car. Add to that the cost of supplies, bunker construction, batteries, boots, knives, and other paraphernalia, and it becomes a fairly expensive proposition.

More expensive in a psychic sense is the commitment to training, to the expertise one needs to be equal to the demands of the post-holocaust environment. Every good general knows you cannot train troops to expertise over a period of months, and then just leave them in garrison somewhere. The edge dulls, morale deteriorates quickly, and the men become restless. And the hard-core Survivalist groups do, in fact, see themselves as elite troops, trained for an imminent war.

Every year that passes without Armageddon increases the frustration level in people who are none too stable to begin with. And every year, as the magic date of A.D. 2000 draws closer, more and more of these people probably will succumb to the temptation to nudge things along just a bit, to help out the apocalypse, to advance the timetable.

In a society as technologically complex and vulnerable as ours, a group of fanatics determined to push us toward societal chaos can do a fearful amount of damage. One of the favorite fantasy-scenarios in the Survivalist literature involves a terrorist strike, by chemical means, that lays waste to America's big cities. It does not require tactical nukes to destroy a city (although there is a remote possibility that some fool could build one of those, too). All it takes is something quick and nasty inserted into the main water supply one dark night.

When a federal strike force raided the fortified Ozark encampment of an outfit called The Covenant, the Sword, and the Arm of the Lord (CSA — get it?), one of the things they found (along with the gun shop where the Ingram that killed Alan Berg had been converted to full-automatic) was a thirty-gallon supply of raw cyanide. One drop of it was more than enough to kill an adult. Imagine what thirty gallons could do if dropped into the water supply of Washington, D.C.

We live, indeed, in times of fear, complexity, and confusion, and our responses to these conditions are colored by a pervasive feeling of impotence. Wickedness is seen to go unpunished on every hand. There is something deeply alluring about the idea of just starting over, wiping the slate clean, and being able to point to those less prudent than ourselves and say: "Hey, I told you so!"

Reinforced anticipation of that day of reckoning brings to the surface all the raw, inchoate anger that many people feel at their inability to influence, or even comprehend, the world they live in.

There have been plenty of other times, and other societies, which both feared and were fascinated by the concept of a total collapse, of the idea that a vast wrecking ball was swinging down from outer space and making way for the ultimate urban renewal project. But historically, the traditional response to such crises has been a group reaction: migrations, the founding of new colonies, building up the castle walls. The American response to the prospect of end-time has been a mutation of the whole folklore myth of the rugged frontier individualist: Grab your gun and head for the hills, men, 'cause the waters are rising!

But what is the Survivalist reflex, really, except surrender-in-advance, turning your back on the possibility of making changes? Why experience the maiming frustration of social work or political activism when the cleansing nuclear fire will take care of all those messy conundrums in, literally, a flash? Why give a damn about the

212

urban poor if you're sitting pretty in a fortified compound in Nebraska with half a million rounds of ammo and a ten-year supply of food?

Hard-core Survivalism is not a positive response to the perils and challenges of the times we live in. For those who submit to its false doctrines and its illusory comforts, it becomes a kind of moral narcotic. As time goes on, it requires heavier and heavier doses of fantasy-actualization to produce the same "high" of certainty and righteousness.

That's why we end up reading about people like Gordon Kahl, the Posse Comitatus leader who stopped paying income taxes in 1970, and who held off dozens of heavily armed lawmen before dying in an inferno of exploding ammunition in a 1983 shootout in Arkansas. Or to Jim Jenkins and his son Steve, who lost their small Minnesota farm to bank foreclosure and who responded, after a failed hard-scrabble attempt to start life over again in another state, by ambushing and killing the bank president and his chief loan officer with assault rifles.

To those reading this in the comfort of a suburban home, Jim and Steve Jenkins may seem like nothing more than cold-blooded murderers. To a middle-aged farmer in Idaho, whose family has been on the land for three generations, who doesn't know how to do anything else but farm, who's in debt to his eyeteeth to a bank that sold him a bill of goods ten years ago and treats him like cow flop today, a man who knows that same kind of banker may come down the road tomorrow, or next week, to forclose on his own property, Gordon Kahl and Jim Jenkins might very well look like authentic American folk heros.

The years between now and the mystical 2000 are going to be increasingly dangerous. The Survivalist groups are growing larger and the conditions which generate their recruits are growing worse. The number of violent incidents involving Survivalists is going to increase. Every year that goes by without the apocalypse just increases their frustration and scorches their synapses a little blacker.

And every year that goes by draws us closer to that watershed of a millennium. If the Apocalypse is really going to happen on that date, then time is really growing short for these people. Caught between the inexorable march of history and the increasing psychic demands of their own fantasies, we can expect a lot of marginal survival types to go over the edge between now and then.

Don't take these people lightly. There are more of them than is generally realized, and their numbers are growing daily. They are fueled by hate-drenched ideologies, manipulated and led by skilled demagogues, preached to by persuasive racist fanatics, and they are armed to the teeth.

And large numbers of them, just like Fritz Klenner, are slowly going mad.

The Family Arsenal

After Fritz Klenner's Blazer exploded just outside of Greensboro on June 3, 1985, throwing weapons and survival equipment in all directions, police raided and searched Fritz and Susie's Greensboro apartment, the Klenner family farm in Reidsville, and Doctor Frederick Klenner's former Reidsville clinic. Following is a partial inventory of the weapons, equipment, and supplies they found:

From the Blazer:

1 Smith & Wesson .22-caliber Magnum revolver
1 Browning .25-caliber automatic pistol
1 Sig-Sauer 9mm automatic pistol
1 Heckler and Koch P2A1 flare gun
1 Colt .45-caliber automatic pistol (Mark IV; Gold Cup National Match version)
1 Heckler and Koch .308-caliber semiautomatic assault rifle
2 Ithaca 12-gauge pump shotguns
1 Uzi 9mm submachine gun

In the Friendly Hills apartment:

1 Steyr 5.56mm assault rifle
2 Ruger .22-caliber carbines
1 Springfield survival rifle, over/under model, .22-caliber and 410-gauge shotgun 2 Remington 20-gauge shotguns
2 Colt .45-caliber automatic pistols
1 Colt Cobra .22-caliber revolver
1 .25-caliber automatic pistol
5 survival knives of various types

1 combat knife with shoulder-holster sheath
1 commando-type knife with ankle holster
Assorted martial arts weapons, including spikes and throwing stars
Assorted extra holsters, ammo cases, magazines, and fast-reload
   clips, all calibers
1 container of Mace with holster
1,262 rounds of 5.56mm ammunition
6,725 rounds of .22-caliber ammunition
150 rounds of .308-caliber ammunition
720 rounds of .45-caliber ammunition
1,250 rounds of 9mm ammunition
129 rounds of .25-caliber ammunition
514 rounds of 20-gauge ammunition
10 rounds of 410-gauge ammunition
Cash totaling $1,219
14 ten-ounce bars of silver
118 one-ounce bars of silver
Assorted gold Krugerands, gold and silver coins, and precious-metal
   jewelry
2 camouflage vests
3 bulletproof vests
1 gas mask
2 canteens
1 first-aid kit
At the Klenner family farm:
6 shotguns
5 semiautomatic rifles
7 pistols
1 machine gun
1.5 cases of dynamite
28 pounds of black powder
2 live Claymore mines
15 tear gas grenades
20 smoke grenades

Note: The Colt AR-15 assault rifle that was used to murder Delores and Jane Lynch was not found among Fritz Klenner's belongings. Fritz sold the weapon sometime after the killings, and police traced it to the new owner.